Davidic Millennialism

Davidic Millennialism

A New Paradigm

Jeffrey Jon Richards

Foreword by Kurt Richardson

WIPF & STOCK · Eugene, Oregon

DAVIDIC MILLENNIALISM
A New Paradigm

Copyright © 2025 Jeffrey Jon Richards. All rights reserved. Except for brief quotations in critical publications or reviews, no part of this book may be reproduced in any manner without prior written permission from the publisher. Write: Permissions, Wipf and Stock Publishers, 199 W. 8th Ave., Suite 3, Eugene, OR 97401.

Wipf & Stock
An Imprint of Wipf and Stock Publishers
199 W. 8th Ave., Suite 3
Eugene, OR 97401

www.wipfandstock.com

PAPERBACK ISBN: 979-8-3852-1025-1
HARDCOVER ISBN: 979-8-3852-1026-8
EBOOK ISBN: 979-8-3852-1027-5

VERSION NUMBER 08/25/25

Where indicated, Scripture quotations are taken from The Holy Bible, English Standard Version. ESV® Text Edition: 2016. Copyright © 2001 by Crossway Bibles, a publishing ministry of Good News Publishers.

Contents

Foreword by Kurt Richardson | vii

Introduction | 1
    Purpose | 1
    Methodology | 8
    Content | 8

Chapter One: Classical Dispensationalism | 10
    History of Dispensationalism | 10
    C. I. Scofield: Structure and Prophetic Vision | 13
    The Second Advent and Kingdom | 15
    Scofield's Views on Free Will, Grace, and Judgment | 15
    Distinction Between Law and Grace | 16
    Scofield's Distinction Between the Kingdom of God and the Kingdom of Heaven | 20
    Lewis Sperry Chafer: Theology and Legacy | 20
    Dispensational Scheme | 24
    Distinctions Among the Dispensations | 25
    Other Theologians of Classical Dispensationalism | 29
    Method of Interpretation | 33
    Select Biblical Passages | 36
    Influence of Classical Dispensationalism | 49
    Conclusion | 53

Chapter Two: Progressive Dispensationalism | 56
    Origin of Progressive Dispensationalism | 56
    Key Theologians | 58
    The Issues | 62
    Interpretations | 64
    Critique of Progressive Dispensationalism | 78
    Conclusion | 83

Chapter Three: Interpretations of the Kingdom | 85
    Historic Interpretations of Classical Dispensationalism | 85
    Select Passages | 95
    The Church and the Kingdom of God | 100
    Conclusion | 106

Chapter Four: Toward a Reconciliation of Views | 109
    Strengths and Weaknesses of Classical Dispensationalism | 109
    Strengths and Weaknesses of Progressive Dispensationalism | 114
    Call for a Future Interpretation | 117
    Conclusion | 120

Conclusion | 123

Bibliography | 129

Foreword

JEFFREY JON RICHARDS's *Davidic Millennialism: A New Paradigm* presents a compelling and carefully constructed reappraisal of contemporary eschatological discourse. At its heart, the work seeks to revisit and reframe the enduring debate over the meaning of the biblical "kingdom"—a question that remains central to the theological understanding of Jesus' mission and message in the New Testament. By focusing especially on the contrast between classical and progressive dispensationalism, Richards not only clarifies an area of frequent misunderstanding but offers a constructive proposal for moving beyond entrenched divisions.

The study begins with a historical and theological overview of classical dispensationalism, a system of thought developed and popularized by figures such as John Nelson Darby, C. I. Scofield, and Lewis Sperry Chafer. Classical dispensationalism envisions the kingdom as a future, literal thousand-year reign of Christ on earth—a reign strictly distinct from the present age of the church. This interpretation maintains a sharp division between God's covenantal dealings with Israel and those with the church, positing the latter as a temporary, parenthetical phase until the prophetic promises to Israel are ultimately fulfilled.

By contrast, progressive dispensationalism—emerging in the late twentieth century through the work of Darrell Bock, Craig Blaising, and Robert Saucy—proposes a significant refinement of this framework. Without discarding key dispensational insights, progressive theologians suggest that the kingdom has already been inaugurated spiritually through Christ's exaltation and current reign at the right hand of God. This perspective affirms continuity between Old and New Testament covenants and envisions the church not as an interruption but as an integral part of God's unfolding redemptive plan. In this view, Christ's present reign is a partial but real fulfillment of the Davidic covenant, to be consummated fully in the eschaton.

Richards sets out to clarify the essential contours of both approaches without caricature or polemic. He further outlines how these perspectives relate to other millennial positions in Christian history: Augustinian amillennialism (which interprets Christ's reign as a present, spiritual reality); postmillennialism (which expects a golden age of gospel expansion prior to Christ's return); and historic premillennialism (which envisions Christ's return initiating a literal reign, apart from dispensational frameworks). While these broader views are addressed for context, Richards's primary focus remains the refinement and reconciliation of dispensational thought.

A major contribution of the book is its methodological integrity. Rather than relying on reactive critique, Richards adopts a constructive posture, engaging major theologians and biblical texts on their own terms. He privileges primary sources and scriptural exegesis, allowing each system to present itself fully before comparison or synthesis is attempted. This respectful and even-handed approach allows readers from across the theological spectrum to engage the discussion on its merits.

In the central chapters, Richards traces the development of kingdom interpretations from the church fathers to Reformation and modern theologians. He devotes particular attention to Augustine's spiritualization of the millennium, which shaped Western eschatology for centuries. Later Reformed theologians, especially at Princeton (such as Charles Hodge and B. B. Warfield), further internalized this view, combining amillennial and postmillennial elements. These contrasts provide a valuable backdrop against which the unique contributions of dispensationalism can be appreciated.

Chapter 3 presents a rich comparative analysis of classical and progressive readings of central kingdom texts, such as the Sermon on the Mount and Jesus' kingdom parables. Where classical dispensationalists traditionally confined these teachings to the future millennium, progressive interpreters find real-time relevance—seeing in them the marks of a kingdom already present yet not fully realized. Richards deftly articulates how progressive dispensationalism affirms both inaugurated and future dimensions of Christ's reign, highlighting how it reframes the Davidic covenant as a living theological reality.

In chapter 4, the book advances a bold and constructive thesis: the proposal of "Davidic Millennialism" as a renewed paradigm that integrates the strengths of both classical and progressive approaches. This terminology, Richards argues, offers a more theologically coherent and biblically grounded framework by emphasizing the centrality of the Davidic covenant. It avoids some of the historical baggage associated with "dispensationalism" while maintaining a firm commitment to the literal fulfillment of God's promises to Israel and the church in a unified eschatological vision.

"Davidic Millennialism" thus functions as both a clarifying term and an ecumenical gesture. It recognizes Christ's current heavenly reign as a real, spiritual enthronement upon David's throne, with a yet-future consummation in his literal return and global kingdom. Drawing on 2 Sam 7 and 1 Cor 15, Richards argues persuasively that this two-phase understanding aligns with the trajectory of biblical revelation and brings needed balance to dispensational theology.

The work's academic rigor is matched by its pastoral sensitivity. Richards is keenly aware of how these theological distinctions affect preaching, worship, ecclesiology, and Christian mission. His call for theological reconciliation is not merely theoretical—it is rooted in a desire to see believers united around the person and reign of Christ, even as they differ on secondary matters of prophetic detail.

In sum, *Davidic Millennialism: A New Paradigm* is a timely and judicious contribution to contemporary evangelical theology. It neither retreats into nostalgic retrenchment nor surrenders to fashionable revisions. Instead, it exemplifies a careful, scripturally faithful, and theologically generous approach to one of the most contested areas of Christian doctrine. By proposing a fresh paradigm that honors the richness of the Davidic covenant while responding to current scholarly and pastoral concerns, Richards has offered a valuable resource for theologians, pastors, and students alike.

His proposal is not merely a middle ground—it is a forward-looking vision for a renewed eschatological hope, grounded in the kingship of Christ and the faithfulness of God's covenantal promises.

Kurt Anders Richardson, DTh
Institute for Abrahamic Relations

Introduction

Purpose

THIS BOOK EXAMINES THE contrasting views of the kingdom as contained in the New Testament. The concept of the kingdom is not clearly distinguished between the two eschatological views of classical dispensationalism and the newly-revised view known as progressive dispensationalism. This work will explore the distinctions, considering both the continuity and discontinuity of the interpretations of what constitutes the New Testament word *kingdom*.

In the Gospels, Jesus proclaims repeatedly, "The kingdom of God is near. Repent and believe the good news!" (Mark 1:15); and "Let the little children come to me, and do not hinder them, for the kingdom of God belongs to such as these. I tell you the truth, anyone who does not receive the kingdom of God like a little child will never enter it" (Luke 18:16); Matthew records, "Jesus went throughout Galilee, teaching in their synagogues, preaching the good news of the kingdom" (Matt 4:23). The apostle Paul also wrote of the topic of the kingdom in Romans, Galatians, Ephesians, Colossians, First Thessalonians, Second Thessalonians, and Second Timothy.

What is this kingdom? Kingdom implies a reign of a royal person—a sovereign who has subjects who are subordinate to an ultimate authority, either willingly or unwillingly. The biblical context is that those who are being ruled comply with the mandates that have been established. The biblical context also suggests that this will be a state of peace devoid of war, hatred, and any demonic interference. Is this kingdom literal or spiritual? Jesus said in Luke 17:21, "Because the kingdom of God is within you," which implies the latter—that the kingdom is spiritual. However, dispensationalism has interpreted the kingdom as primarily physical, lasting a literal one-thousand years in duration. Erickson believes "the rule of Christ will be complete from the very beginning of the millennium. Evil will have been virtually eliminated." Erickson continues, "Dispensationalists hold to a continuing unconditional covenant of God with national Israel, so that when God has completed his dealings with the church, he will return to his relations with national Israel."[1] Ryrie gives a concise classical dispensational view of a literal, physical millennium:

> After the second advent of Christ, the millennial kingdom will be set up in fulfillment of all the promises given in both Testaments and particularly those contained in the Abrahamic and Davidic covenants. The Lord Jesus Christ, who will personally take charge of the running of the affairs of the world during that age, will be the chief personage of the dispensation. It will continue for a thousand years, and man will be responsible for obedience to the King and His laws. Satan will be bound, Christ will be ruling, righteousness will prevail, overt disobedience will be quickly punished. Yet at the end of the period enough rebels will be found to make a formidable army that will dare to attack the seat of government (Rev 20:7–9). The revolt will be unsuccessful, and the rebels will be cast into everlasting punishment.[2]

Though it is common to ignore the topic of the kingdom, which usually is a subdivision of eschatology, Rowland emphasizes the importance of the kingdom to eschatology:

> Eschatology has been central to most interpretations of the ministry of Jesus as presented in the synoptic Gospels in the biblical interpretation of the last century or so. According to the Gospel of Mark, Jesus' first words are "the time is fulfilled; the kingdom of God is at hand; repent and believe in the gospel" (Matt 1:15). The phrase "the kingdom of God" is a central pillar for our understanding of the message of Jesus. It probably refers to the future age of glory, when the divine will would be revealed in human affairs. Eschatological understanding of the kingdom of God has dominated New Testament scholarship throughout the bulk of the last century. The Matthean version of *The Lord's Prayer*, with its petition that God's kingdom would come and his will be done on earth as in heaven (Matt 6:10) is an accurate exposition of the

---

1. Erickson, *Christian Theology*, 1217–18.
2. Ryrie, *Dispensationalism*, 64–65.

essential features of the Jewish belief concerning the eschatological and this-worldly character of the kingdom. Luke 11:20 and 17:21 offer evidence of a present anticipation of the coming eschatological kingdom, in which the eschatological age was already at work in Jesus' ministry.[3]

There have been many temporal kingdoms throughout history that followed the course of rise, expansion, and decline. Some of the major ones have been the Babylonian, Persian, Roman, Mongolian, and British Empires. These kingdoms were accomplished through military power and the subjugation of vast territories and diverse populations. While their expansion and acquisition of power were impressive, there was not true peace and justice during the reigns of those in power. For example, the reigns of Roman emperors were often short-lived, marked by distrust, political rivalries, and even familial assassinations. The pursuit of power, territorial expansion, control, and wealth was typically the driving force behind efforts to conquer and subjugate various peoples and nations.

The Christian understanding of the interpretation of the kingdom is in stark contrast in most respects to the temporal, human, historical kingdoms. This kingdom has been interpreted essentially as either spiritual or material. The Augustinian view, adopted by a large segment of Christianity, understands the kingdom as either the reign of Christ within the church or the saints reigning with him in heaven. This position has been given the designation amillennial and is perhaps the dominant millennial view in Christendom, particularly among the Roman Catholic Church and many mainline Protestant denominations in the United States. However, the human condition has made this position difficult for some to embrace. Wars, pandemics, and widespread religious apathy seem to contradict the idea that the kingdom is currently in effect. Despite these challenges, the topic of the kingdom remains significant, as it intersects with many of the major Christian doctrines such as theology proper, Christology, pneumatology, hamartiology, ecclesiology, and anthropology.

The postmillennial position is vastly different from either the amillennial or premillennial views. According to Grudem, "The 'millennium' that postmillennialists hold to is *very different* from the 'millennium' the

---

3. Rowland, "Eschatology," 58–59. Rowland states his belief that eschatology has been the central concern of most interpretations in the last century of the ministry of Jesus as revealed in the Synoptic Gospels; Benedict Vivano agrees, citing as his sources both E. P. Sanders's *Jesus and Judaism* and D. C. Allison's *Jesus of Nazareth: Millenarian Prophet*. Vivano, "Quest for the Historical Jesus," 85.

premillennialists talk about. In a sense, they are not even discussing the same topic. While premillennialists talk about a renewed earth with Jesus Christ physically present and reigning as King, together with glorified believers in resurrected bodies, *post*millennialists are simply talking about an earth with many, many Christians influencing society."[4] One significant proponent of the postmillennialism was the Princeton theologian Charles Hodge, who writes of the mandate of Jesus:

> Having imposed upon His Church the duty to preach the Gospel to every creature under heaven, he endowed it with all the gifts necessary for the proper discharge of this duty, and promised to send his Spirit to render their preaching effectual. . . . The duties of the ministry, therefore, are to continue until all, that is all believers, the whole Church, or, as our Lord says, all the elect, are gathered in and brought to the perfection in Christ.[5]

The postmillennial view declined significantly in the twentieth-century, largely due to historical realities such as the two world wars and the Great Depression. Grudem gives a long discourse that, in his opinion, the world is becoming more filled with evil.[6]

Dispensational premillennialists believe that Christ will reign on earth for one thousand years, establishing the true kingdom—unlike any prior kingdom in history. This era will be characterized by peace, and the curse on nature will be lifted. Thus, ecological issues—particularly those of the past century—will no longer be concerns, as even the natural order will be subject to the sovereign reign of Christ.

Despite its significance, eschatology has often been regarded as less central than doctrines as Christology and pneumatology. Walls believes,

> Given the integral place that eschatology has in the structure of Christian belief, and given that a substantive eschatology is essential for a credible theology, it is more than a little note-worthy that it has not always enjoyed the attention and prominence that it deserves. Indeed, we need only look at the twentieth century to see a period when Christian theology lost its nerve, and consequently eschatology did not receive due consideration. . . . In much academic theology of that era, Roman Catholic as well as

---

4. Grudem, *Systematic Theology*, 1122–23 (emphasis original).
5. Hodge, *Systematic Theology*, 801.
6. Grudem, *Systematic Theology*, 1124.

INTRODUCTION

Protestant, eschatology was little more than an appendix to systematic theology.[7]

Karl Barth argues that Protestant theology has largely neglected eschatology, to its detriment. He writes that most Protestant theologies have succeeded in putting us "comfortably to sleep by adding at the conclusion of Christian Dogmatics a short and perfectly harmless chapter entitled—'Eschatology.'"[8]

Walls gives an overview of the three major millennial views:

> One long-standing controversy in eschatology that illustrates the variety of interpretive options . . . concerns the meaning of the millennium in Revelation 20. . . . A hallmark of dispensationalism is the belief that the final dispensation is the millennium, a literal thousand-year reign of Christ that will occur after his Second-Coming. Dispensationalism is the best-known version of the position called premillennialism, the view that the return of Christ will initiate an extended period of peace and justice on earth before the final judgment, but not all who hold to this position are dispensationalists. A second option held by many classical theologians and prominent contemporary scholars is known as amillennialism. The essence of this view is that Christ's millennial reign has already been inaugurated through his death and resurrection and the coming of the Holy Spirit. The millennial reign is thus an invisible one that is presently manifested in the church and that will be brought to fulfillment when Christ comes in glory for all to see. A third prominent position is postmillennialism, which maintains that the millennium will come as a result of progressive growth of the kingdom, culminating in the entire world being converted to Christ, after which he will visibly return. Other variations on these three main options are possible, but these three highlight the fact that mainstream interpreters have read the Apocalypse in very different ways.[9]

The purpose of this book is not to survey the historical development of alternate views of the millennium; thus, a discussion of their origins, interpretations, and theological controversies within and among the three

---

7. Walls, *Handbook of Eschatology*, 7.
8. Barth, *Epistle to the Romans*, 500.
9. Walls, *Handbook of Eschatology*, 13.

will not be included. Instead this work pertains to a discussion of the kingdom within classical dispensationalism and progressive dispensationalism.

Interest in the millennium—also referred to as chiliasm or millenarianism—remains strong in the twenty-first century. Throughout church history, many have speculated on just what Jesus meant when he announced, as found in Luke 10:9, "The kingdom of God has come near to you." The apostle Paul using the same Greek word, *basileia* (βασιλεία), in Romans 14:17 states, "For the kingdom of God is not a matter of eating and drinking but of righteousness and peace and joy in the Holy Spirit." Immediately the text raises questions such as, Is this a spiritual kingdom? Who qualifies for inclusion in this reign? Who is ruling in this kingdom? When does the kingdom begin, and does it have an end?

For many, the topic of the kingdom falls within the theological doctrine of eschatology—the study of future events, history's culmination, and the ultimate destiny of creation. Certainly, this is a topic of interest both universally and individually, especially as political leaders vie for more financial and military security for their respective countries and coalitions. Moreover, recent global crises, including the COVID-19 pandemic and wars in Europe and the Middle East, have also raised questions about the prospect of the kingdom.

Rather than surveying all patristic literature on the subject, this work focuses on a specific interpretation that continues to be well known both in academic communities and on a popular level. The early church, until the time of Augustine in the fourth and fifth centuries, understood the kingdom in what is now termed historic premillennialism—that is, the kingdom of which Christ spoke will be established literally on earth for one thousand years, but such a kingdom will not occur until after the second advent of Christ. Those who adhere to historic premillennialism interpreted literally various Old and New Testament passages as foretelling a worsening world condition before the return of Christ. This view is seen in the writings of Justin Martyr, Irenaeus, Hippolytus, Tertullian, and Lactantius. The second advent, then, with Christ's literal coming, will vanquish evil forces and the kingdom will be established after which the eternal state will commence.

Over time, Augustine's view became known as amillennialism, and over the centuries, it has been the dominant method of interpreting texts about the kingdom, which is believed to have commenced with the first advent of Christ and will continue until the second advent when the last conflict will occur. The death and resurrection of Jesus assured that demonic forces were defeated; however, there is obviously still an abundance of evil that is very much part of humanity's daily experience. Christ reigns in the hearts of individual believers, and departed saints are eternally and blissfully in God's presence. The Reformers such as Luther and Calvin were all heavily influenced by Augustine's eschatological stance. In America, most mainline denominations in the United States hold to this view, including Presbyterianism, Lutheranism, and Methodism.

Beyond historic premillennialism and amillennialism, a third millennial position emerged and gained traction, particularly in the past few decades. Daniel Whitby (1638–1726) is cited as the founder of this view, known as postmillennialism. This optimistic perspective holds that, through the progressive triumph of the gospel, world conditions will gradually improve, culminating in Christ's second coming. However, historical catastrophes—such as the Great Depression and World War II—led to a significant decline in the acceptance of postmillennialism, and today, only a small number of theologians continue to hold this view.

John Nelson Darby is usually credited with systematizing a theological position referred to as dispensationalism. He influenced such theologians as C. I. Scofield and Lewis Sperry Chafer. Dispensationalism is premillennial; however, this position differs in many aspects from historic premillennialism, though both hold that the second coming of Christ will occur before the millennium that will be a literal one-thousand-year reign of Christ on earth.

In the mid-1990s, a revised theological framework, known as progressive dispensationalism, began to replace the traditional Darby-Scofield-Chafer position. Classical dispensationalism appeared to these scholars to be somewhat misguided and even out of date. Notably, progressive dispensationalism introduced several theological shifts that bear similarities to amillennialism, particularly in relation to the kingdom of God.

Three scholars in particular—Darrell Bock (a recent Humboldt Scholar at Tübingen), Craig Blaising, and Robert Saucy—have written extensively on progressive dispensationalism. Each of these theologians holds an academic position in postgraduate theological institutions, and their work will be examined in this study. Specifically, their perspectives will be compared and contrasted with classical dispensationalism, focusing on how the concept of the kingdom has evolved within contemporary theological discourse.

Many seminaries and denominations within Protestantism in the United States hold to either classical or progressive dispensationalism as their primary method of theological interpretation. Select biblical passages and interpretations as well as a variety of theologians will be examined to determine if classical and progressive dispensationalism have incited major changes in the interpretation of the concept of the kingdom.

Methodology

This study will undertake a critical examination of both classical and progressive dispensationalism, focusing on key interpreters within each theological framework. Particular attention will be given to how these scholars critique the concept of the kingdom.

An inductive approach will be employed—that is, allowing the sources and interpretations to speak for themselves. Since the book's purpose is not to contrast dispensationalism vis-á-vis other systems such as Reformed, charismatic theologies, Wesleyan, and other positions, critics of dispensationalism will not be cited as extensively.

Many of the sources, especially for classical dispensationalism, are historical since this persuasion has been extant for many decades. By contrast, progressive dispensationalism is a more recent development; therefore, its sources and discussions will reflect contemporary theological discourse.

Content

This book consists of four chapters. Chapter One, "Classic Dispensationalism," is a survey of major dispensational theologians. A brief history of the origins of dispensationalism and significant writers and their methods of interpretation will be discussed. Some of them are well known and had widely acclaimed ministries, whereas others did not. Central biblical passages and their interpretation will be explored. Many of the theologians were well versed in the biblical languages, so attention is given to exegesis and the method of hermeneutics.

Chapter Two, "Progressive Dispensationalism," will begin by presenting the origins of the new theological movement and the theologians of progressive dispensationalism who are actively involved in research. Some of the major issues will be compared as well as the methods of interpretation.

INTRODUCTION

Of course, there are criticisms of both stances, and some of these will be articulated.

Chapter Three, "Interpretations of the Kingdom," examines historical interpretations of the kingdom. This will include other views such as amillennialism, postmillennialism, and historic premillennialism. Select Old and New Testament passages will be explored with attention given to exegetical interpretations and considerations. Contemporary interpretations of the kingdom will also be examined.

Chapter Four, "Toward a Reconciliation of Views," discusses the strengths and weaknesses of classical dispensationalism, examining the method of interpretation. Progressive dispensationalism's revision is appraised. There is a critique of both their strengths and weakness and suggestions for other considerations for interpretations. The classical view has been for many years the sole means of interpreting the kingdom; this view is seen in the work of three persons who are usually cited as the primary historic theologians of this position: John Nelson Darby, C. I. Scofield, and Lewis Sperry Chafer. Up until the mid-1990s, there were only slight modifications in their views of the dispensations and the kingdom. Beginning in the mid-1990s, a significantly revised position began to be taken seriously, which subsequently came to be known as progressive dispensationalism.

Chapter One

Classical Dispensationalism

History of Dispensationalism

THE CONCEPT OF THE kingdom is not clearly distinguished between the two eschatological views of classical dispensationalism and its newly revised counterpart, progressive dispensationalism. This work explores the key distinctions between these views, considering both continuity and discontinuity in their respective interpretations of the New Testament concept of the kingdom.

If a particular theological stance does not originate with the church fathers —such as Augustine—or with the Reformers, including Calvin, Luther, or Melanchthon, it is often met with skepticism by some theologians. This is certainly the case with the theological persuasion known as dispensationalism. The word dispensation is translated from the Greek word οἰκονομία, which, according to the Nestle-Aland Greek New Testament, is translated "management of a household," "responsibility," or "plan."[1] One of the primary arguments against dispensationalism is its relatively recent origin in church history—that is, the method of interpretation is not believed to have been seen in the writings in the early centuries of the church.

Usually John Nelson Darby (1800–1882) is commonly cited as the originator of dispensationalism. After graduating from Trinity College,

---

1. Aland et al., *Greek New Testament*, 124.

Dublin, he was admitted to the bar but relinquished his legal career after receiving a call to ministry. He initially served as a clergyman in the Church of England but resigned his position as a priest and eventually joined the Plymouth Brethren Church.[2]

He held to a seven-dispensation framework, believing that Scripture delineates seven distinct economies in God's redemptive plan: Paradise, Noah, Abraham, Israel, Gentiles, Spirit, and Millennium.[3] Dispensations and their duration are explained by Darby as follows:

> This however we have to learn in its details, in the various dispensations which led to or have followed the revelations of the incarnate Son in whom all the fulness was pleased to dwell.... The detail of the history connected with these dispensations brings out many interesting displays, both of the principles and patience of God's dealings with the evil and failure of man; and of the workings by which He formed faith on His own thus developed perfections. But the dispensations themselves all declare some leading principle or interference of God, some condition in which he has placed man, principles which in themselves are everlastingly sanctioned of God, but in the course of those dispensations placed responsibly in the hands of men for the display and discovery of what he was, and the bringing in their infallible establishment in Him to whom the glory of them all rightly belonged.... In every instance, there was total and immediate failure as regarded man, however the patience of God might tolerate and carry on by grace the dispensation in which man has failed in the onset; and further, that there is no instance of the restoration of a dispensation afforded us, though there might be partial revivals of it through faith.[4]

Many argue, however, that dispensationalism did not originate in later centuries within the church but that its foundational elements can be identified in the ante-Nicene fathers, including Justin Martyr (110–65), Tertullian (160–220), and Victorinus of Petau (d. 304). Each theologian compiled a basic history extending from Adam to the millennium.[5]

Arnold D. Ehlert compiled an extensive bibliography on dispensationalism and traced the concept of dispensations back to the six days of creation and the seventh day of rest in Genesis. He argues that these six

---

2. Ryrie, *Dispensationalism*, 77.
3. Darby, *Collected Writings*, 2:568–73.
4. Darby, *Collected Writings*, 1:192–93.
5. Ice, "Dispensationalism."

days of creation serve as a prophetic model, prefiguring six historical ages followed by utopia, the final period of rest.

Ehlert cites David Gregory of Oxford, who believes the Hebrew letter aleph, appearing six times in Gen 1:1, holds numerical significance in Jewish tradition. Since, in Jewish arithmetic, aleph represents one thousand, Cabalistic scholars concluded that the world would last six thousand years, culminating in a seventh millennium of rest. Ehlert further references several church fathers, whom he concludes as affirming the importance of this six-thousand-year framework, followed by a final sabbatical era.

From the time of the Reformation, Ehlert examines the writings of William Gouge and Pierre Poiret, arguing that a dispensational scheme appear in their writings. He also contends that John Edwards wrote the first extensive work on dispensationalism and that Jonathan Edwards in his *History of the Work of Redemption* articulates a form of dispensational thought.

J. N. Darby later developed a seven-part dispensational scheme, however, in terminology his system differs significantly from later dispensationalists such as C. I. Scofield. Other writers whom Ehlert believes hold to a dispensational scheme are Robert Jamison, James H. Brookes, Robert Cameron, James M. Gray, William Evans, and H. A. Ironside.[6]

This early framework is commonly termed "classical dispensationalism" and was studied and promoted on an academic level as well as a popular one. However, beginning in the mid-1990s a major revision of classical dispensationalism occurred. Robert G. Clouse gives insight into this dramatic shift:

> The move away from the traditional classic dispensationalism of Cyrus Scofield and Lewis Sperry Chafer caused conservative adherents of the view to become extremely upset. . . . The eschatological view of major scholars such as Oscar Cullman with its emphasis on the "already but not yet" hermeneutic and the tension between the inauguration and the realization of the kingdom informed their outlook on the definition of the church and the place of Israel in the present age. Whereas classic dispensationalism held that Israel and the church were two distinct peoples of God, these new scholars rejected the "two people of God" teaching and the notion that the church is a parenthesis in the plan of God. Despite these differences, the progressives continue to believe that Israel will be restored to God's favor, that Christ will return to establish

---

6. Ehlert, "Dispensationalism."

his millennial reign on earth, and that the church will be raptured, thus escaping the great tribulation.[7]

There are other areas of differences between classical and progressive dispensationalism that continue to cause strong disagreement within the ranks of those who hold to a dispensational method of interpretation. This is especially true of those older scholars who regard classical dispensationalism's method of interpretation as that which is the only legitimate one.

C. I. Scofield: Structure and Prophetic Vision

C. I. Scofield, more so than John Nelson Darby, influenced the dissemination of dispensational theology. Scofield was born in Michigan in 1843. A voracious reader from childhood, he initially planned to attend the University of Virginia; however, the Civil War intervened, and he served for four years in the Confederate Army, where he was awarded the Confederate Cross of Honor.

Following the Civil War, he moved to St. Louis to study law and finished his studies in 1869. He became involved in politics, twice serving as a representative in the Kansas State Legislature before being appointed as U.S. district attorney for Kansas. In 1882 Scofield transitioned to ministry, becoming the pastor of a Congregational Church in Dallas, Texas, where he served until 1887. By 1895, Scofield was called to serve as the pastor of Trinitarian Congregational Church of Northfield, Massachusetts, and simultaneously appointed president of the two Northfield preparatory schools, the East Northfield and Mount Hermon Schools founded by D. L. Moody. He continued in these positions until 1902 when he resigned to return to Dallas to again pastor where he had served from 1882–87. During his second pastorate in Dallas, Scofield founded the Central American Mission.[8]

Scofield insists that Israel and the church must always remain distinct. He describes the differences among the church, Israel, and the gentiles:

> It should be needless to say that, in this dispensation, neither Jew nor Gentile can be saved otherwise than by the exercise of that faith on the Lord Jesus Christ whereby both are born again (John 3:3, 16) and are baptized into that "one body" (I Cor 12:13) which

---

7. Clouse, "Fundamentalist Theology," 275.
8. Scofield, *Rightly Dividing*.

is the "Church" (Eph 1:22, 23). In the Church the distinction of Jew and Gentile disappears (1 Cor 12:13; Gal 3:28; Eph 2:14). So in writing to the Ephesians the Apostle speaks of them as "in times past Gentiles" (Eph 2:11; I Cor. 12:2).[9]

Scofield holds to a seven-dispensation scheme. He asserts:

> The Scriptures divide time (by which is meant the entire period from the creation of Adam to the "new heaven and new earth" of Revelation 21:1) into seven unequal periods, usually called "dispensations" (Eph 3:2), although these periods are also called "ages" (Eph 2:7) and "days"—as, "day of the Lord," etc.
>
> These periods are marked off in Scripture by some change in God's method of dealing with mankind, in respect of two questions: of sin and of man's responsibility. Each of the dispensations may be regarded as a new test of the natural man, and each ends in judgment—marking his utter failure in every dispensation.
>
> Five of these dispensations, or periods of time, have been fulfilled; we are living in the sixth, probably toward its close, and have before us the seventh, and last—the millennium.[10]

These seven dispensations include Innocence, Conscience, Government, Promise, Law, Grace, and Kingdom.

He maintains that the present time is the period of grace, which, according to his interpretation, began with Jesus' death and eliminated the binding nature of the law. But like all dispensations, or specific periods of time, this age too will end in failure, resulting in judgment upon an unbelieving world and an apostate church.

The divine event that will close this present dispensation, according to Scofield, will be the descent of the Lord from heaven to take up the church with himself into the heavens, and this event he called the "rapture" of the church. A period of seven years called the "tribulation" will occur, and after this time the personal return of the Lord, or the second coming of Christ, will take place. With the commencement of the millennium, Israel will be restored, and the Lord will reign over the earth for one thousand years. Scofield believes that the seat of authority will be at Jerusalem, and the church along with the saints of the period of grace will be associated with him.

At the end of the one-thousand-year reign, Satan, having been bound, will be released to deceive the nations, leading them into battle against

---

9. Scofield, *Rightly Dividing*, 6.
10. Scofield, *Rightly Dividing*, 12.

the Lord and his saints. This battle will end in victory for the Lord and his armies. The Great White Throne Judgment will take place, and all the wicked dead will be raised and judged. After this event, the eternal state will commence.[11]

The Second Advent and Kingdom

Scofield holds to two advents. The first is Christ's birth and is consummated in his death and resurrection. He did not divide the second coming into a coming for the saints and a coming with the saints. He apparently only designated a general second coming; the taking up of the saints and a return with them are both included in his understanding of the "second coming."

He also affirms that the Scriptures teach two resurrections: "Two resurrections, differing in respect of time and of those who are the subjects of the resurrection, are yet future. These are variously distinguished as 'the resurrection of life' and 'the resurrection of damnation,' or as the resurrection of the just and the unjust."[12]

Scofield's Views on Free Will, Grace, and Judgment

Scofield is more in line with Calvinist theology rather than Armenian or Wesleyan theology. Calvinism emphasizes God's sovereignty and humanity's total dependence on God's grace as revealed in Christ, whereas Wesleyan theology emphasizes prevenient grace and human free will, teaching that individuals determine their eternal destiny through their choices. Poythress gives insight into the central themes of Scofield's theology.

> What views does Scofield offer us in his notes of his reference Bible? First of all, they are evangelical. They are mildly Calvinistic in that they maintain a high view of God's sovereignty. Scofield affirms the eternal security of believers and the existence of unconditional promises. Moreover his emphasis on the divine plan for all history would naturally harmonize with a high view of God's sovereignty.[13]

---

11. Scofield, *Rightly Dividing*, 26.
12. Scofield, *Rightly Dividing*, 26.
13. Poythress, *Understanding Dispensationalists*, 20.

He cites Rev 20:4–6 as teaching that the first resurrection applies only to those who "sleep in Christ," while the second resurrection occurs one thousand years later and includes the unbelieving dead. 1 Thess 4:13–16, according to Scofield, further supports this doctrine. Summarizing his position, he writes: "The testimony of Scripture, then, is clear that believers' bodies are raised from among bodies of unbelievers, and caught up to meet the Lord in the air a thousand years before the resurrection of the latter. It should be firmly held that the doctrine of the resurrection concerns the *bodies* of the dead. Their disembodied spirits are instantly in conscious bliss or woe."[14]

Scofield rejects the concept of one general judgment, arguing instead for five distinct judgments:

> "The expression 'general judgment', of such frequent occurrence in religious literature, is not found in the Scriptures. . . . The idea intended to be conveyed by that expression is not found in the Scriptures."[15]

According to Scofield, these five judgments are as follows: (1) the judgment of the believer that took place on the cross; (2) the judgment of sin in the believer, which can take place anytime; (3) the judgment of the works of believers, which will occur when Christ comes again, the results of which will be reward or loss of reward; (4) the judgment of nations, which takes place at the close of the tribulation and occurs in the vicinity of the Valley of Jehoshaphat; and (5) the judgment of the wicked dead, or the Great White Throne Judgment. The latter judgment, according to Scofield, will take place sometime after the millennium, and the result is separation from God.[16]

Distinction Between Law and Grace

The relationship of the Old Testament to the New Testament was a subject of great concern to Scofield. He holds to the distinction between law and grace:

> It is, however, of the most vital moment to observe that Scripture never in any dispensation, mingles these two principles. Law always has a place and work distinct and wholly diverse from that

---

14. Scofield, *Rightly Dividing*, 28 (emphasis original).
15. Scofield, *Rightly Dividing*, 28.
16. Scofield, *Rightly Dividing*, 28–33.

CLASSICAL DISPENSATIONALISM

> of grace. Law is God prohibiting and requiring. Grace is God beseeching and bestowing. Law is a ministry of condemnation; grace of forgiveness. Law curses, grace redeems from that curse. Law kills; grace makes alive.... Everywhere the Scriptures presents law and grace in sharply contrasted spheres. The mingling of them in much of current teaching of the day spoils both; for law is robbed of its terror, and grace of its freeness.[17]

Scofield emphasizes that the law by itself cannot justify a person. He asserts that the era of the law began at Sinai and extended to Calvary, serving only to expose human helplessness in the face of sin. In contrast, he teaches that faith in Christ establishes a unique relationship between the believer and God in the present age of grace.

Essential to this period of grace is the church, which, according to Scofield, is not found in any previous dispensation. "The Church apart from the prophetic word, 'I will build my church' (Matt 16:18), remained a 'mystery hid in God' (Eph 3:9, 10). The unfolding of that mystery was reserved to the Apostle Paul, to whom was also entrusted the exposition of the doctrine of grace (Eph 3:1–10)."[18]

In his *Addresses on Prophecy*, Scofield argues that the church is found only in the New Testament since its beginning is seen in Acts 2 and its consummation is portrayed in the fourth chapter of First Thessalonians.[19] Reformed theology finds the church in the Old Testament and does not make a distinction between Israel and the church; Scofield repeatedly denies the Reformed view of comingling the two. He consistently writes remarks such as the following: "Why should we suppose then that all good people through all ages, were members, and are members of the church? As a matter of fact, they were nothing of the kind."[20] Scofield believes that the church was unknown to Old Testament prophets. It was a period of indeterminate time. He believed that the Gospels, Matthew, Mark, and Luke, pertain to the church only in a secondary sense.[21] "Christ is never called King of the Church. 'The King' is indeed one of the divine titles, and the Church in her worship joins Israel in exalting 'the King, eternal, immortal, invisible' (Ps. 10:16; 1 Tim. 1:17). But the Church is to reign with Him. The Holy Spirit

---

17. Scofield, *Rightly Dividing*, 34–55.
18. Scofield, *What Do the Prophets Say?*, 102–3.
19. Scofield, *Addresses on Prophecy*, 21.
20. Scofield, *Addresses on Prophecy*, 32.
21. Scofield, *Scofield Reference Bible*, 990.

is now calling out, not the subjects, but the co-heirs and co-rulers of the kingdom."[22] Scofield emphasizes that the church is only a "pilgrim" in a world that is not consonant with the purposes of God. "What in a word, is the relation of the church to the world? Briefly this: to pass through it a pilgrim body of witnesses."[23]

In his eschatological framework, Scofield places significant emphasis on the fulfillment of biblical prophecy as evidence of divine inspiration:

> Fulfilled prophecy is a proof of inspiration because the Scripture predictions of future events were uttered so long before the events transpired that no merely human sagacity or foresight could have anticipated them, and these predictions are so detailed, minute, and specific as to exclude the possibility that they were mere fortunate guesses.[24]

Prophecy, then, serves as a means of validating the divine origin of Scripture. Furthermore, he insists that biblical prophecy must be fulfilled literally, rejecting symbolic or allegorical interpretations.

What was the purpose of prophecy for Scofield? Prophecy serves to instill confidence in those who await the Lord's return.[25] He understands the study of prophecy as a systematic process: "My task is to gather into orderly sequence the testimony of the Holy Spirit, through the prophets."[26]

Scofield interprets 2 Pet 1:21 as evidence that the prophetic message people articulated came from God. He places great emphasis on the prophecy found in Dan 9, which details the seventy weeks in the prophetic calendar. According to Scofield, sixty-nine of these weeks have already been fulfilled, while the seventieth week remains future, corresponding to the tribulation period.[27]

Scofield places the seventy weeks into three segments: (1) seven weeks, which in the prophetic calculations is equal to forty-nine years; (2) sixty-two weeks, which corresponds to 434 years; and (3) the week which is to be a seven-year period. He claims that the first seven weeks or forty-nine years were fulfilled from the decree to the actual rebuilding of Jerusalem. This decree, which is found in Neh 2, is understood by him to be during

22. Scofield, *Scofield Reference Bible*, 990.
23. Scofield, *Addresses on Prophecy*, 25.
24. Scofield, *Scofield Reference Bible*, 1318.
25. Scofield, *Addresses on Prophecy*, 90.
26. Scofield, *Addresses on Prophecy*, 56.
27. Scofield, *Scofield Reference Bible*, 914–15.

the twentieth year of the reign of Artaxerxes, or in 445 BCE. The decree is understood to be the initial point of calculating the sixty-nine weeks as they relate to the cutting off of the Messiah. The last week, or the seventieth week, Scofield claims, is still future and alludes to the tribulation period on earth, during which the church will be in the presence of God. Scofield writes, "When the Church-age will end, and the seventieth week begins, is nowhere revealed. Its duration can be but seven years. To make it more violates the principle of interpretation already confirmed by fulfillment."[28] Between the sixty-ninth and seventieth week, he asserts, is the present age of grace.

During this seventieth week, Scofield asserts that a leader who opposes God—identified as the Antichrist—will rise to power. He interprets Dan 9:27 as predicting this figure, writing:

> "The 'he' of verse 27 (Dan 9) is the 'prince that shall come' of verse 26, whose people (Rome) destroyed the temple, AD 70. He is the same with the 'little horn' of chapter 7. He will covenant with the Jews to restore their Temple sacrifices for one week (seven years), but in the middle of that time, he will break the covenant and fulfill Dan 12:11 and 2 Thess 2:3, 4."[29]

Scofield claims that this antichrist and his work are depicted also in 2 Thess 2:3 and 4 and in Matt 24:15. He will be energized supposedly by satanic powers, and his purpose is to destroy the church and establish his own evil empire.

Scofield contends that biblical prophecy is primarily concerned with the seventh dispensation, the millennium, also termed the kingdom. He emphatically asserts, "The kingdom was no mystery. The kingdom is the great theme of the prophets. From Isaiah to Malachi the burden of the prophetic testimony is the kingdom to be set up by the Messiah, David's great Son, but who was to be also 'the mighty God, the Everlasting Father.'"[30]

He repeatedly describes the millennial period as not as an age of grace but as an era of righteousness.[31] During this time, the King will reign, and Satan will be bound. Scofield identifies this reign as the fulfillment of the Davidic covenant, in which the Davidic dynasty will be fully established.[32]

28. Scofield, *Scofield Reference Bible*, 914.
29. Scofield, *Scofield Reference Bible*, 914–15.
30. Scofield, *Addresses on Prophecy*, 70.
31. Scofield, *Addresses on Prophecy*, 378.
32. Scofield, *Addresses on Prophecy*, 66.

He is definitive concerning the initiation of the millennial period. Repeatedly he states that this period will begin immediately after the seven-year period of tribulation. Scofield claims that the form of government will be a theocracy.[33] Jesus will reign as the ultimate monarch during this thousand-year period.

Scofield's Distinction Between the Kingdom of God and the Kingdom of Heaven

Interestingly, Scofield distinguishes between the phrases "kingdom of God" and "kingdom of heaven." "The 'kingdom of God' is a great inclusive expression, which occurs in the whole sphere where God rules. The 'kingdom of heaven' is the establishment, through Christ, of God's righteous reign on earth, it is always limited to the earth, . . . though glorified saints of this and past ages are concerned with it."[34]

Scofield teaches that the disciples originally preached the "kingdom of heaven," but because this message was rejected, the kingdom was postponed. As a result, God is now calling out His own through the church. He identifies Matt 11 as a pivotal chapter marking the Jewish rejection of the gospel of the kingdom.[35] He asserts that the phrase "kingdom of heaven" is found only in the Gospel of Matthew.[36] The principles of the kingdom are specified, he states, in the Sermon on the Mount. The passage, therefore, has only a secondary reference to the present church age. Many of the parables relate both to the kingdom of heaven and the kingdom of God, but he emphasizes that they primarily refer to the former, or to the kingdom of heaven.

Lewis Sperry Chafer: Theology and Legacy

Born in Rock Creek, Ashtabula County, Ohio, on February 27, 1871, Lewis Sperry Chafer was the son of Reverend Thomas Franklin Chafer and Lois Lomira Sperry. Thomas graduated from Auburn Theological Seminary with the class of 1864 and was the local congregational minister. He was

---

33. Scofield, *Addresses on Prophecy*, 113.
34. Scofield, *Addresses on Prophecy*, 105.
35. Scofield, *Scofield Reference Bible*, 1011.
36. Scofield, *Scofield Reference Bible*, 998.

born in 1828 and lived until 1882. His father, William Chafer, was born in York, England, and came to the United States in 1837. Lois Lomira Sperry was born in Rock Creek, Ohio, in 1836 and lived until the fall of 1915. Her father, Asa Sperry, was a licensed Welsh preacher. Her maternal grandmother of Irish descent was Ann Sperry.[37]

Following his father's death, Chafer's mother moved the family to Oberlin, Ohio, with the intention of providing her son with an opportunity for education at Oberlin College. He attended Oberlin from 1889–92. The college was founded by the revivalist Charles G. Finney; Sydney Ahlstrom writes of Oberlin as a "center of influence for revival theology."[38]

In 1903, the Chafers relocated to East Northfield, Massachusetts, and Lewis was affiliated with Northfield from 1903–9. During these years, the Northfield Bible Conference featured such biblical expositors and theologians as H. W. Webb-Peploe, G. Campbell Morgan, W. Graham Scroggie, and F. B. Meyer of Great Britain; W. H. Griffith-Thomas and A. B. Winchester of Canada; and A. T. Pierson, William B. Eerdman, C. I. Scofield, H. A. Ironside, and George Guille of the United States. In later years, Chafer acknowledged the influence of these dispensational, premillennial theologians when he wrote, "The association and close acquaintance with some of the world's greatest expositors . . . placed before me the ideals of expository preaching based on an extended knowledge and familiarity with the Scriptures."[39]

Of all the people Chafer met in his Northfield days, the one who influenced him the most was C. I. Scofield. Chafer often likened this relationship to that which is between a father and son.[40] He left Mount Hermon in 1911, and in the following years he associated with a host of well-known teachers and evangelists, especially R. A. Torrey, W. H. Griffith-Thomas, and G. Campbell Morgan. In 1912, through the influence of James Sprunt, a board member of the Union Theological Seminary in Richmond, Virginia, Chafer delivered a message at the seminary. The student body of Union Seminary apparently responded very favorably to Chafer since they wrote a letter to James Sprunt concerning Chafer's message, which in part read,

> It was a continual feast of spiritual blessing the full value of which is inestimable. Judging from the remarks made by members of each

---

37. Lincoln, "Biographical Sketch," 4.
38. Ahlstrom, *Religious History*, 1:558.
39. Chafer, "Twenty Years of Experience."
40. Chafer, "Dr. Scofield," 120.

class in our student body we have not been favored with a series of lectures more deeply spiritual, more edifying and more inspiring than these which have been our recent privilege to enjoy. A profound impression has been made upon the students of the impelling force of true expository preaching, which is true preaching.[41]

Chafer writes of the dispensations of law, grace, and kingdom in his book *Satan*. Concerning the kingdom period, he wrote, "There is still a more extensive body of Scripture which anticipates a literal kingdom of righteousness and peace upon earth. This theme was the burden of the Old Testament prophets, and was announced by John the Baptist, by Christ, and his disciples."[42] He emphasizes in this book that the present age will not witness the kingdom:

> Again this age is not the earthly kingdom for nowhere are the promised conditions of that kingdom now to be found. The Old Testament prophecies contained long and detailed descriptions of that glorious time. God's ancient people shall become the chosen nation, restored to their own land; the enemy shall be banished; the earth shall be purified, and blossom as a rose.[43]

Published in 1911, *True Evangelism* was written in 1901; *The Kingdom in History and Prophecy* was published in 1915. Chafer gave some interesting opinions concerning how the kingdom has been interpreted in some divisions of Christendom:

> A clear and thoroughly Biblical book on the kingdom in the Scriptures has long been a *desideratum*. Perhaps no truth of divine revelation has suffered more at the hands of interpreters than that concerning the kingdom. Following the Roman Catholic interpretation, Protestant theology has very generally taught that all the kingdom promises, and even the great Davidic covenant itself, are to be fulfilled in and through the church.[44]

In 1922, Chafer published Grace, a work often regarded as one of his most important theological contributions. The book was written with dispensational distinctions emphasized throughout the work. Primarily he distinguishes among the dispensations of law, grace, and kingdom, yet

---

41. Crane et al. to James Sprunt, Dec. 7, 1912, Dallas Theological Seminary archives, quoted in Renfer, "Dallas Theological Seminary," 94.

42. Chafer, *Satan*, 26–27.

43. Chafer, *Satan*, 36.

44. Chafer, *Kingdom*, 5.

he portrays the operations of grace in each of the three periods. Chafer's premillennial eschatological views are also apparent in this work: "The Bible affords no basis for the supposition that the Lord will come to a perfected social order. At his coming He will gather the saved to Himself, but the wicked He will judge in righteousness. The transcendent glory of this age which will have been either accepted or rejected."[45]

In 1926, Chafer wrote *Major Bible Themes*. These forty-six chapters express what he believes are key emphases in the Scriptures. He wrote the *Ephesian Letter* in 1935. His last work, *Dispensationalism*, was completed in 1951. Also, during this academic period of Chafer's life, he wrote articles for *The Sunday School Times*, *Our Hope*, *Moody Monthly*, and *The King's Business*. However, the most prominent means through which Chafer expressed his theological and doctrinal views was the *Bibliotheca Sacra*.

The crowning literary achievement, and in many respects the primary achievement of Lewis Sperry Chafer's life, was his eight-volume *Systematic Theology*. The first systematic theology written from a dispensational, premillennial position, his *Systematic Theology* was the culminating work of many years of writing and organizing themes and doctrines. The initial step toward the completion of the *Systematic Theology* entailed the systematizing of his lectures in theology into outlines. He then published for his students three analytical questionnaires. Walvoord writes, "Most sections were laboriously written in longhand twice before being committed to his faithful secretary, Mr. A. H. D. Duncan for typing.[46]

Chafer, in 1934, wrote of the need for a theology written from a dispensational, premillennial position in an article entitled "Unabridged Systematic Theology," which was published in the *Bibliotheca Sacra*. Soon after the publication of the *Systematic Theology*, in 1948, Clarence Mason wrote,

> To those of us who hold a dispensational position this theology is greeted with enthusiasm and gratefulness. At last we have something codified, knit together in a logical unit, and in full enough compass to state adequately the Scriptural basis of our position. Many fine things have been said, scattered through many fine books; many fine sermons have been preached; but very little of this has been available to the average reader and, certainly, nothing as satisfying as this in codified form.[47]

45. Chafer, *Grace*, 149.
46. Walvoord, "Lewis Sperry Chafer," 869.
47. Mason, "Thrilling Theology," 535. Lynn Landrum, a journalist in the '40s and '50s, not only in Dallas but throughout the state of Texas, writes after having received a set of

Walvoord wrote in a similar manner: "The appearance of the eight-volume work in *Systematic Theology* by President Lewis Sperry Chafer of Dallas Theological Seminary is without question an epoch in the history of Christian doctrine. Never before has such a work similar in content, purpose, and scope been produced."[48]

Dispensational Scheme

Chafer wrote the *Systematic Theology* over a period of eleven years, 1937–48. The order of topics are as follows: bibliology, theology proper, angelology, anthropology, hamartiology, soteriology, ecclesiology, eschatology, Christology, and pneumatology. He gave his rationale for the writing of the work:

> It is therefore contended that an unabridged treatment of theology is needed. To cover the ground completely, a doctrinal summary has been added to this work in which more than a hundred doctrines not found in a systematic treatment of theology are analyzed.
>
> Why premillennial? So far as the author knows the present work is the only one approaching theology from an orderly and logical interpretation of the Scriptures. The supreme value of this interpretation will be observed, it is believed, as one pursues this work.
>
> Why dispensational? Apart from a sane recognition of the great purposes and time-periods of God, no true understanding of the Bible has ever been received.

---

the *Systematic Theology*, "Think of it! Eight big volumes presented by the author as a gift to a working newspaperman—and every word of it about systematic theology. You do not need to be told that Lewis Sperry Chafer believes that theology is the most important thing to which he could possibly devote his time. These eight volumes are his life work. Did you ever think about God, about His universe, about how sin and salvation got into this world and about what goes on in the next world? Stop now, just for an experiment, and ask yourself where is the starting point in thinking of that sort. The chances are you will give up before you get started. Well, Lewis Sperry Chafer did not give up. And this unabridged work is a monument to his industry, to his analytical powers, to his amazing facility in fitting passages together, so that one throws light on the other.... But when you stop to savor what Dr. Chafer is saying, you come to the realization that we have here one of the outstanding stylists among religious writers of the day. Dr. Chafer's sentences neither strut nor stumble. They march with orderly purpose and yet not without grace. In writing, he is a 'workman that needeth not to be ashamed.'" Landrum, "Thinking Out Loud." Cf. Moody, "Present Theological Trends," 9–11.

48. Walvoord, review of *Systematic Theology*, 115.

CLASSICAL DISPENSATIONALISM

When systematic theology includes the premillennial and dispensational interpretations of the Bible, much added material is discovered and the work is greatly extended.[49]

In *The Kingdom in History and Prophecy*, Chafer gives in outline form many of the themes later seen in the *Systematic Theology*. He writes of the kingdom as prophesied in the Scriptures, the kingdom offered and rejected, the present age of grace, the church, the succession of kingdoms as predicted by Daniel, the Olivet Discourse, the second advent, and the millennium itself. All these themes are in essential agreement with his mature eschatology as contained in the *Systematic Theology*. Concerning the second advent, Chafer believes that attention to this doctrine, especially from pastors, will bring rejuvenation to a lethargic church.[50]

Chafer is representative of classical dispensationalism. How does he understand this theological position? He sees specific periods in the Bible which he calls "dispensations." In his work, *Dispensationalism*, which is an outgrowth of an article published in 1936 in the *Bibliotheca Sacra*, he understands the word "dispensation" as derived from the Latin *dispensatio*, which is translated "economic arrangement" or "superintendence." The Greek equivalent is *oikonomia*, which is generally translated as "stewardship" or "economy."[51]

Distinctions Among the Dispensations

Chafer held to seven distinct dispensations: The dispensation of innocence extended from the creation to the fall. The dispensation of conscience spanned from the fall to the flood. The third era of human government extended from the flood to the call of Abraham, while the dispensation of promise spanned from the call of Abraham to the giving and receiving of the Mosaic law. The fifth era, law, continued from the giving and accepting of the law until the death of Christ. Interestingly, Chafer believes that this age will be reinstituted again in the future. He believed that this is the seventieth week of Daniel and is future to the present age. The sixth and present dispensation he believes is that of grace, or the age that extends from the death of Christ until his return to receive the bride or the church. He

---

49. Chafer, *Systematic Theology*, 1:xxxvii–xxxviii.
50. Scofield, introduction to *Kingdom*, 6.
51. Chafer, *Dispensationalism*, 8.

explains the grace age by the following: "It is an age characterized by grace in the sense that in this age, God, who has always acted in grace toward any and all of the human family whom He has blessed, is now making a specific heavenly demonstration of His grace by and through the whole company of Jews and Gentiles who are saved by grace through faith in Christ."[52]

The seventh and last dispensation, according to Chafer, will be that of the kingdom. It will be a period of one thousand years and will end with the creation of a new heaven and a new earth. What will distinguish this period? It is characterized by the facts that Satan is bound, the covenants of Israel are fulfilled, creation is delivered from its bondage, and the Lord himself will reign over the earth and on the throne of David.

These seven dispensations comprise Chafer's dispensationalism. He essentially only emphasizes law, grace, and kingdom. Two of these apply solely to Israel:

> Quite apart from the revealed will of God as recorded of earlier ages, the Bible sets forth at length three distinct and complete divine rulings which govern human action. None of these rulings are addressed to angels or to the Gentiles as such. Two are addressed to Israel—one in that age that is past, known as the Mosaic law, and the other the setting forth of the terms of admission into, and the required conduct in, the Messianic kingdom when that kingdom is set up on the earth. The third is addressed to Christians and provides divine direction in this age for the heavenly people who are already perfected with respect to standing, in Christ Jesus.[53]

Chafer contends that the Mosaic law was specifically designed to govern Israel in the land and was an interim form of government, described in Exod 19 to the coming of Christ. He believes that the apostle Paul writes of the purpose of the law in Gal 3, stating that the purpose is to stress the insufficiency of human works and the need for God's grace through Christ.

Chafer realizes that "like the teachings of the law of Moses, the teaching of grace has not applied to men in all ages. These teachings were revealed from God through Christ and His apostles."[54] When Chafer writes about the present age of grace and its benefits, he emphasizes its universal scope:

---

52. Chafer, *Systematic Theology*, 1:41.
53. Chafer, *Dispensationalism*, 45.
54. Chafer, *Grace*, 147.

> There is but one issue in this dispensation between God and the unregenerate man, and that is neither character nor conduct; it is the personal appeal of the gospel of the grace of God. Until the unsaved receive Christ, who is God's gift in grace, no other issue can be raised. Men may moralize among themselves, and establish their self-governments on principles of right conduct; but God is never presented in the unfoldings of grace as seeking to reform sinners. Every word regarding the quality of life is reserved for those who are already related to Him on the greater issue of salvation.[55]

Chafer writes of three specific features of the age of grace. First, he speaks of the independent character of this age. The age of grace, he claims, extended from the death of Christ until the translation of the church. It is called grace because during this period God, as revealed in his Son, demonstrated his grace in bringing salvation to both Jew and gentile.[56] This present age is a mystery, and Chafer defines this term as "some work or purpose of God hitherto unrevealed. It may be related to something which needs to be understood but have a key."[57] He believes that the present age was unanticipated by the Old Testament prophets. They saw the first and second comings of Christ but not the intervening age between these two events. Whereas the dispensations of law and kingdom are characteristically legal, the church age is distinguished by grace. Thus, the age of grace is independent of law and kingdom. Under grace, it is recognized that Christ has died, is risen and ascended, and the Holy Spirit resides in the hearts of God's redeemed.

Second, he speaks of the exalted requirements of this age. He sees the standard of life under grace as actually higher than what was required under the law:

> It may be well stated again that the standard of conduct prescribed under the teachings of grace is immeasurably more difficult to maintain than that prescribed either by the Law of Moses, or the law of the kingdom.... Turning to the Scriptures which reveal the position and responsibility of the child of God under grace, it is found that a *superhuman* manner of life is proposed.[58]

---

55. Chafer, *Systematic Theology*, 4:183.
56. Chafer, *Systematic Theology*, 1:41.
57. Chafer, *Systematic Theology*, 7:240.
58. Chafer, *Systematic Theology*, 4:186 (emphasis original).

But Chafer, thirdly, writes of divine enablement. He claims that there is supernatural power for the child of God. "Under grace, the all-powerful, abiding, indwelling and sufficient Holy Spirit of God is given to every saved person. . . . The superhuman manner of life under grace is not addressed to some spiritual company alone within the whole body of Christ; it is addressed to all believers alike."[59] Inherent in the age of grace is a compassionate God who, though not unmindful of sin in his own, lovingly showers his favor upon his recipients. There is hope for believers to live a victorious life. "If the manner of life under grace is supernatural, so, also, the provided enablement is supernatural, and is as limitless as the infinite power of God. Since God has proposed a humanly impossible manner of life, He has, in full consistency, provided the Spirit who giveth life."[60]

The kingdom age is the third period to which Chafer devotes much thought. The elements of the dispensation of grace are absent in the kingdom age. He states,

> The third administration which is contained in the Bible is that which is designed to govern the earthly people in relation to their coming kingdom. It is explicit, also, with regard to the requirements that are imposed upon those who enter the kingdom. The body of Scripture is found in the Old Testament's portions which anticipate the Messianic Kingdom and in large portions of the Synoptic Gospels.[61]

Although Chafer holds to a seven-dispensation scheme, rarely does he write of the seven as a unit. Rather, he writes primarily of the dispensations of law, grace, and kingdom. Each one is a distinct time period, and each has conditions imposed upon it by God.

To clarify his thinking on dispensationalism, Chafer specifies what he believed a true dispensationalist is:

> What persons, then, according to these definitions, should be classified as a dispensationalists? The answer to this question may be stated in a variety of ways. Three of these may suffice: (1) Any person is a dispensationalist who trusts in the blood of Christ rather than bringing an animal sacrifice. (2) Any person is a dispensationalist who claims any right or title to the land which God covenanted to Israel for an everlasting inheritance. And (3) any

---

59. Chafer, *Systematic Theology*, 4:188.
60. Chafer, *Systematic Theology*, 4:190–91.
61. Chafer, *Dispensationalism*, 50.

person is a dispensationalist who observes the first day of the week rather than the seventh. To all this it would be replied that every Christian does these things, which is obviously true that, to a very considerable degree, all Christians are dispensationalists.[62]

Both Scofield and Chafer are key representatives of classical dispensationalism. They influenced greatly dispensationalism for many years; in particular, the *Scofield Reference Bible*, with its detailed interpretive notes, popularized Scofield's views. Meanwhile, Chafer's eight-volume Systematic Theology served as a course text in colleges, seminaries, and other academic settings for decades. With the revised position, usually termed "progressive dispensationalism," classical dispensationalism came to be seen as outdated and lacking key components. Debate continues between adherents of both positions.

Other Theologians of Classical Dispensationalism

Several other dispensationalists were active during the Scofield-Chafer era, though they were not as influential as their contemporaries. C. H. Mackintosh (1820–96) was a premillennialist who believed in two resurrections, according to Rev 20:5–6. He believed that there is one before the thousand-year period and the second is after this period of time. He wrote of a resurrection and a translation of the saints:

> All the saints of God, both those of Old Testament and New Testament times who lie sleeping in our cemeteries and graveyards, or in the ocean's depths—all these would rise from their temporary sleep. All the living saints would be changed in a moment, and all would be caught up to meet their descending Lord, and return with Him to the Father's house (John 14:3; 1 Thess 4:16–17; 1 Cor 15:51–52).[63]

Mackintosh claims that the Scriptures identify three classes of people: the Jews, Gentiles, and the church of God.[64] Mackintosh clearly adheres to dispensational premillennialism, with little distinction between his eschatology and that of Scofield and Chafer.

---

62. Chafer, *Dispensationalism*, 9.
63. Mackintosh, *Mackintosh Treasury*, 871.
64. Mackintosh, *Mackintosh Treasury*, 886.

William L. Pettingill (1886–1950) was a consulting editor of the 1909 edition of the *Scofield Reference Bible* and had thoroughly dispensational views. Like Chafer, Pettingill is adamant that the church and the kingdom cannot be identical.[65] In his writings, Pettingill discusses the return of the Lord after the tribulation period, the judgment of the nations, and the last judgment itself.[66] His eschatological views are almost identical to those of Scofield and Chafer.

William Kelly (1821–1906) was a Plymouth Brother who also held to a pre-tribulation translation of the church. He stresses that there will be a gospel of the kingdom that will be preached in the time of the tribulation. This gospel, he believes, is not identical with the gospel of grace that is being preached during the present dispensation of grace.[67] Kelly describes in detail the judgment of the nations and the conditions for entrance into the kingdom. He places great emphasis on the lordship of Christ during the kingdom reign:

> Satan's getting power over man was only a fearful interruption, but not one whose consequences the Lord could not overmaster and purge out: He means to do it; and to have this world the scene of incomparably greater blessedness than its present misery is through Satan's work. God means to give the kingdom of this world to His son—yea, He will have the universe put under Christ.[68]

The only difference between Kelly and Scofield and Chafer lies in their writing style; the three were in essential agreement on theological matters.

E. Schuyler English, though a dispensationalist and premillennialist, does not emphasize—as Scofield and Chafer did—the significance of the covenants. The fact that both Scofield and Chafer stress the fulfillment of the covenants promised to Israel give cohesiveness to their thought and establishes a thread of unity between the two testaments; however, English did not. Overall, English espouses the traditional dispensational, premillennial interpretation:

> It is our conclusion, however, that the translation of the saints, the rapture of the Church, will occur before any portion of the Tribulation, Daniel's seventieth week, takes place. And it is our further conviction that once the truth of this is seen, all difficulties vanish

---

65. Pettingill, *Simple Studies in Matthew*, 269.
66. Pettingill, *Simple Studies in Matthew*, 291–98.
67. Kelly, *Lectures on Matthew*, 440.
68. Kelly, *Lectures on Matthew*, 482.

CLASSICAL DISPENSATIONALISM

and all Scripture that pertain to the subject fall into place in such a way as to complete a perfectly clear and beautifully concise picture of God's dealing with His Church.[69]

H. A. Ironside (1876–1951), a well-known dispensational premillennialist, describes the physical conditions of the millennium in a more vivid manner than either Scofield or Chafer:

> All that is lovely, such as the grandeur of Lebanon, the beauties of Carmel and Sharon's plains will be retained in that new era, and to these will be added many additional testimonies to the Creator's joy in the world which He brought into being by the word of His power, but which has been terribly marred as a result of man's sin. Every fruitful field and orchard, every lovely garden, presents a foretaste of what in Messiah's day will be everywhere prevalent, when the parched deserts will give place to meadows.[70]

Marsden honors Ironside by recognizing him as the pastor of Moody Church in Chicago.[71] In Ironside's *Not Wrath but Rapture*, he argues for the translation of the saints before the commencement of the tribulation period. Ironside believed,

> There are in fact two distinct stages of our Lord's return presented in the New Testament. This is the rapture which precedes the great tribulation. He is going to be manifested with all His saints when He descends to exercise judgment on those who have persisted in rejecting His grace, and when He will set up His glorious kingdom to reign in righteousness over the world. In other words, while the Old Testament and the four Gospels, together with other scriptures, plainly predict Christ's second coming to establish His kingdom on this earth, it is part of the mystery hidden from past ages that when He comes, He will have with Him a Bride to share His throne, as well as a host of other redeemed saints from all past dispensations in His train.[72]

There are only minor differences among Scofield, Chafer, and Ironside in their eschatological positions.

A. C. Gaebelein (1861–1945) was a dispensationalist and was a close associate of C. I. Scofield. He was editor of the millenarian periodical *Our*

---

69. English, *Re-Thinking the Rapture*, 122.
70. Ironside, *Isaiah*, 217–18.
71. Marsden, *Fundamentalism*, 95.
72. Ironside, *Not Wrath but Rapture*, 43.

Hope and was also a consulting editor of the *Scofield Reference Bible*. He convened a major Bible conference in Carnegie Hall, New York City, from November 25–28, 1918, which, according to Sandeen, attracted large crowds.[73]

Gaebelein wrote *The Revelation*, describing the book of Revelation as "the capstone of the entire revelation of God, without which the Bible would be an unfinished book, [noting] we find in its pages the consummation of the great Prophecies which were given by the Prophets of God in the Old Testament times."[74] He also wrote the book *The Prophet Daniel* and understood the book of Daniel as intimately connected with the book of Revelation, which he believed to be the only prophetic book in the New Testament. He believed that the prophetic portions of Daniel would remain sealed if we did not have the book of Revelation.[75]

In his work *The Conflict of the Ages*, he speaks of what he considered to be the certainty of prophecy:

> The Bible forecasts the future. Its forecasts are sure and certain beyond the shadow of even the remotest doubt. History proves it. Hundreds of years before certain empires came into existence, The [sic] Bible predicted their coming and what should come to pass. This we find in the prophecies of Daniel. Other prophets of God foretold the fall and ruin of Babylon and Nineveh, when these cities were flourishing and in the zenith of their power. . . . Still more striking is the pre-written history of the people of Israel. The fact no infidel has ever been able, nor will be able, to answer. Fulfilled prophecy demonstrates the Bible as the infallible Word of God.[76]

Gaebelein writes concerning the prospect of knowing matters pertinent to the future: "We can know the future through the Bible, the Word of God, but never apart from it. In the pages which follow we shall give some of the most startling facts as to the prophecies revealed in the Scriptures, some of their past fulfillments and the rapidly approaching fulfillment of all prophecy."[77]

---

73. Sandeen, *Roots of Fundamentalism*, 175.
74. Gaebelein, *Revelation*, 10.
75. Gaebelein, *Prophet Daniel*, 5.
76. Gaebelein, *Conflict of the Ages*, 161.
77. Gaebelein, *World Prospects*, 18.

Gaebelein divides the book *World Prospects* into three sections, relating each to the people of Israel, the Gentiles, or the church. This division, of course, reminds one of Scofield's and Chafer's identical divisions.

Method of Interpretation

Classical or traditional dispensationalism has historically interpreted the Scriptures with a strong emphasis upon the historical-grammatical method; this hermeneutical procedure is considered the *sine qua non* of interpretation, without which it is believed correct interpretation is not possible. In his work *The Kingdom in History and Prophecy*, published in 1915, Chafer forcefully enunciates his conviction concerning the necessity of a premillennial interpretation:

> Accepted inferences of so-called postmillennialism and Premillennialism as possible co-existing systems of interpretation constitute a serious challenge against the dignity and purpose of the Bible itself. Either the divine revelation follows a definite order in the development of the kingdom in the earth, or it does not. If it does, there could hardly be two distinct programs co-existing in the mind and purpose of God.[78]

Additional understanding into his thinking is offered in the following quotation:

> Chiliasm, . . . meaning one thousand[,] refers in a general sense to the doctrine of the millennium, or the kingdom age, that is yet to be; and as stated in the *Encyclopaedia Britannica* is "the belief that Christ will return to reign a thousand years." The distinctive feature of this doctrine is that He will return *before* the thousand years and therefore will characterize those years by His personal presence and by the exercise of His rightful authority, securing and sustaining all the blessings on the earth which are ascribed to that period. The term *chiliasm* has been superseded by the designation *Premillennialism*, and naturally, since Premillennialism is now confronted by both Postmillennialism (only in its literature) and Amillennialism—neither one of which opposing systems could be expressed by the title *Chiliasm*—more is implied in the term than a mere reference to a thousand years. It is a thousand years which is said to intervene between the first and second of humanity's resurrections (Rev 20:4–6); which resurrections are named in 1

---

78. Chafer, *Kingdom in History and Prophecy*, 17.

> Corinthians 15:23–26 as "they that are Christ's at his coming," and "the end" (resurrection). In the Corinthian passage, as in Revelation 20:4–6, these resurrections are separated by a kingdom reign when Christ, according the Corinthian passage, before delivering this kingdom to the Father, shall have put down all rule, and authority and power, and shall have put all enemies under His feet. ... In this thousand years ... every earthly covenant with Israel will be fulfilled—all, indeed, that belongs to the Messianic Kingdom.[79]

Chafer defends premillennialism by citing other scholars who hold to this position, and he refers to the following persons: Bengal, Olshousen, Gill, Stier, Alford, Lange, Lillie, Meyer, Kurtz, Stark, Fausset, Jones, Nast, Delitzsch, Bonar, Ryle, Seiss, and Cunningham.[80]

Chafer perhaps should have been careful to explain that dispensational premillennialism was not the view of the early church. Even though he does not explicitly state that it was, he seemingly gives this impression by articulating:

> Some modern writers seem to realize but little that chiliasm or premillennialism was the all-but-universal belief of the early church, or the extent of that conviction in all centuries when any truth has been received at all. It is hardly worthy of any scholar to assert that this is a modern departure, or, if held in the early centuries, was looked upon as heresy.[81]

Though both Scofield and Chafer hold to a historical-grammatical hermeneutical method and claim that Scripture must be interpreted in accordance with its plain meaning, they also believe that the Scriptures contain phenomenological and figurative language. Regarding Reformed eschatology, Chafer especially is not writing against the fact of symbolism in the Scriptures, but rather against the method of interpretation:

> While some prophecy is couched in symbolic language, those portions which trace the forward movements of the kingdom in the earth are largely free from the problems presented by such symbolism, and that body of truth appears in language and terms the meaning of which cannot reasonably be questioned. The pity is that Origen ever conceived the allegorizing method of interpretation, and that his misleading and violent liberty with the text has

---

79. Chafer, "Introduction to Prophecy," 108–9.
80. Chafer, "Introduction to Prophecy," 132.
81. Chafer, *Systematic Theology*, 4:271.

since found such fertile soil to propagate a mixture of teachings concerning Israel, as a nation, with the revelations concerning the Church, the body of Christ, is groundless in Scripture. It is hopelessly confusing and grotesque, for under this plan only Israel's blessings are borrowed; her curses and penalties are, naturally, not wanted. No progress can be made in the kingdom studies unless plain words are taken in their obviously plain meaning.[82]

At this point, it would be helpful to briefly discuss eschatology's historical development. Ladd, a premillennialist and critic of dispensationalism, offers a helpful summary of the church father's concept of the kingdom:

> In the early church two interpretations of the kingdom are to be found: an eschatological interpretation and a non-eschatological interpretation. During the first two centuries the kingdom of God in the Church Fathers was exclusively eschatological. A typical passage is found in the *Didache*: "Remember, Lord, they Church, to . . . gather it together in its holiness from the four winds to thy kingdom which thou has prepared for it." The Church is the present visible people of God on earth, but the kingdom is the future realm of blessedness to be experienced after the return of Christ to the earth. . . . A survey of the literature leads to the following conclusions. The understanding of the kingdom is exclusively eschatological; and with one exception there is no Church Father before Origen who opposed the millenarian interpretation, and there is no one before Augustine whose extant writings offer a different interpretation of Revelation 20 than that of a future earthly kingdom consonant with the natural interpretation of the language.[83]

Ryrie, a classical dispensationalist, writes that during the medieval period "the doctrine of the kingdom, as held by the early Church, was almost exterminated under the teaching and power of the papacy."[84] Concerning the present period, Ryrie writes, "The modern period has witnessed a mixture of beliefs. First it has seen the rise and fall of postmillennialism. Although its roots may be traced to Augustine, the father of modern postmillennialism is Daniel Whitby. The theory has been outlined and does not have many adherents today. Amillennialism has flourished in the modern era with the weight of such men as B. B. Warfield, L. Berkhof, and O. T. Allis."[85]

---

82. Chafer, *Kingdom in History and Prophecy*, 15.
83. Ladd, *Crucial Questions*, 22–23.
84. Ryrie, *Basis of Premillennial Faith*, 27.
85. Ryrie, *Basis of Premillennial Faith*, 30.

Both Scofield and Chafer wrote and taught during the period in which postmillennialism exerted a great influence. It is difficult to calculate the precise year or period when postmillennialism waned and amillennialism became more prominent.

Chafer, in his introduction to Feinberg's work, writes, "To say that postmillennialism is dead, is not to imply that it does not occupy a large place in historical theology, nor that its theories are not found in theological works which were written in the days when eschatology was handed down practically without change from generation to generation and before the benefits which accrue to it from fresh analyses of Scripture were enjoyed."[86]

Both Scofield and Chafer are convinced that the Reformed eschatological position was not true to the Scriptures. The primary issue dividing dispensational premillennialism and Reformed eschatology was the view of Israel and the church. The promises to Israel of a literal, earthly kingdom are fulfilled by the church, according to Reformed theology. Scofield and Chafer, however, believed that God was pursuing a specific course for Israel and a unique course for the church; therefore, Israel and the church were kept separate in their schemes.

Chafer especially was familiar with the eschatological positions of the Hodges and Warfield. Chafer was an ordained minister within the denomination that considered these three Princeton postmillennial theologians to be of supreme value in the understanding of a Reformed eschatological position. Chafer, in his *Systematic Theology*, does not cite amillennial theologians, but he certainly does cite many postmillennial ones, in particular Charles Hodge, Archibald Hodge, and Benjamin B. Warfield.

Select Biblical Passages

Both Scofield and Chafer understand the seven-year period termed the "tribulation" to be a future event. They believe that the church will be translated into the presence of God before this occurrence. They see the tribulation period as one of the major highways of prophecy that can be traced throughout the Scriptures, and they find this subject in the following passages: Dan 12:1; Matt 24:9–26; 2 Thess 2:1–12; Rev 3:10; and Rev 6:1—19:6.[87] Chafer explains the tribulation period as follows:

---

86. Chafer, forward to *Millennialism*, 9.
87. Chafer, *Systematic Theology*, 7:306.

The great tribulation is the period known as Daniel's seventieth week (Dan 9:24–27), the order of events being the same in Daniel as in Matthew 24 and in 2 Thessalonians 2.

The final week or heptad is seven years in duration, which is proved by the fact that is was exactly 69 x 7 years between the order to rebuild Jerusalem and the cutting off of Messiah. The remaining seventieth "week" of years belongs to Israel's age and will be characterized by the same general conditions as obtained in the past Jewish age. The time will be shortened a little (Matt 24:22). It is known as "the time of Jacob's trouble" (Jer 30:4–7) out of which Israel will be saved. The great tribulation is the time of God's unavoidable judgments on a Christ-rejecting world (Ps 2:5). It is characterized by:

1. The removal of the Holy Spirit together with the church from the earth (2 Thess 2:7).
2. The casting of Satan into, thus restricting him to, the earth (Rev 12:9–12).
3. The development of sin which was hitherto restrained (2 Thess 2:11).
4. The rule of the man of sin (John 5:43).
5. Termination by the second coming of Christ, the battle of Armageddon, and the smiting stone of Dan 2.[88]

The tribulation period, according to both Scofield and Chafer, is a period in which Israel will be chastised; she is to be brought to her knees because of perpetual rejection of Christ as the Messiah. It will be a period of purging in order that she might enter the millennial kingdom. Chafer believes that "at the end of this age, Israel must pass through the great tribulation, which is specifically characterized as 'the time of Jacob's trouble' (Jer 30:4–7; Dan 12:1; Matt 24:21; and, before entering her kingdom, she must come before her king in judgment."[89] According to Chafer, the times of the gentiles will be completed with the end of the seven-year period. How does this period, yet to be experienced, fit into the grand scheme of the purposes of God for Israel?

The tribulation period, yet to be experienced in this world, is the completion of a sequence of predicted years, all of which should intervene between the plucking of Israel off the land, which occurred at the time of the Babylonian captivity, and the final return

88. Chafer, *Systematic Theology*, 7:307.
89. Chafer, *Systematic Theology*, 4:10–11.

of that people to their land in the full realization of their covenanted blessings under the Messiah's reign. But for the intercalary age of the Church, this period is precisely measured at 560 consecutive years, which time is divided into intervals, namely, 70 years of the Babylonian captivity as predicted by Jeremiah (Jer 25:11–12), 49 years in which Jerusalem would be rebuilt (Dan 9:25), 434 years to the cutting off of Messiah (Dan 9:26), and 7 years in which the covenant between the prince and the many will be confirmed. Such is the precise measurement of the Gentile times, though these years are equally laden with events which are Jewish. In the final 7 years the last Roman emperor—the beast—arises, and Gentile times are terminated by the glorious appearing of Messiah. Whatever belongs to the Gentile times began with the Babylonian captivity and aside from the intercalary age of the Church is revived and consummated in the yet future 7 years. . . .

Again, the purpose of the great tribulation is wholly extraneous to the Church. That period is declared to be for the final judgments of God upon a God—and Christ—rejecting world. It is the ending of the *cosmos* system. Over against this, the Church is neither a part of the *cosmos* . . . nor is she ever to be brought into condemning judgment (John 5:24; Rom 8:1). She will be judged relative to rewards which belong to faithful individuals, which judgment is not on the earth but is in heaven, and certainly is no feature of the earthly tribulation. To demand that believers must experience the terrible judgment and destruction which must fall on unbelievers is to do violence to every feature of the saving grace of God.[90]

Both Scofield and Chafer are convinced that only with the visible, personal coming of Christ will the millennium on earth be established for one-thousand years. They did not believe that the preaching of the gospel, science and technology, education, or any other human means will ever initiate this time of perfect order and peace on earth. Chafer believes,

> The Bible teaches that God will ultimately triumph over all sin and rebellion in the earth. This is stated in many passages notably 1 Cor. xv. 24–28: "Then cometh the end, when he shall have delivered up the kingdom to God, even the father; when he shall have put down all rule and authority and power. For he must reign, till he hath put all enemies under his feet. The last enemy that shall be destroyed is death. For he hath put all things under his feet. But when he hath said all things are put under him, it is manifest that he is excepted, which did put all things under him. And when all

---

90. Chafer, *Systematic Theology*, 4:364–65.

things shall be subdued unto him, then shall the Son also himself be subject unto him that put all things under him, that God may be all in all.

Thus does the divine record predict the restoration of the universe to its primal blessedness under the unchallenged authority of God, when the Son shall have put down all authority and banished every foe. This purpose, as recorded in the Bible appears in various stages, or aspects, all leading with the certainty of the Infinite to the glorious consummation.[91]

Both Scofield and Chafer believe that the millennium will begin as a perfect order since only the sheep and not the goats will be allowed to enter this estate. The process of the judgment of the nations will assure this. Chafer writes of what he believed is an error concerning the kingdom: "One of the greatest errors of theologians is an attempt, as essayed now, to build a kingdom on the first advent of Christ as its basis, whereas according to the Scriptures it will be realized only in connection with the second advent. All Scriptures conform to this arrangement, strange though it may look."[92]

Even though the first advent resulted in the atoning death and the victorious resurrection of Christ, sin is still rampant, and this malady of humanity will continue until the second advent takes place. The Church has been anticipating this event for approximately two thousand years, and according to Matt 24:36, only the Father knows the time of the second coming of Christ.

The concept of the Old Testament covenants are important in dispensational theology, especially those of the Abrahamic and Davidic covenants. Rather than being understood as conditional, these two are believed to be unconditional; thus, it is believed that their fulfillment is assured. Concerning the Abrahamic covenant, Abraham's seed was promised to become an everlasting nation. Both Scofield and Chafer believe that though the offer was rejected, God's offer, the promise to Abraham will still occur. The covenant was given in detail in Gen 12, and it is claimed by classical dispensationalists that it will continue to the end of the book of Revelation, which is believed to be yet future, beginning with Rev 4 and continuing through Rev 22. There are other covenants as well, including the Palestinian covenant, which is believed to be contained in Deut 30:3–8, and the Davidic covenant as detailed in 2 Sam 7:16.

---

91. Chafer, *Kingdom in History and Prophecy*, 18.
92. Chafer, *Systematic Theology*, 7:224.

DAVIDIC MILLENNIALISM

The Davidic covenant is especially given high priority in both classical and progressive dispensational thought. Chafer writes,

> Since the coming theocratic kingdom is the divine objective with respect to the earth and since it forms the national hope of Israel, the covenant with David which introduces the revelation of the kingdom declares the precise nature of all this. From the inception of this dominant theme onward as seen in subsequent Scriptures the subject is held in constant observation as a feature of unfulfilled prophecy. This earthly kingdom, the throne, and the King are among the dominant themes of the Old Testament. The revelation respecting these great features in the Davidic covenant is both explicit and extended. Difficulty arises only for those who are determined to metamorphose a literal, earthly throne and kingdom into some vague and wholly imaginary spiritual idealism.[93]

Chafer claims that there is only one reservation concerning the covenant and that pertains to those succeeding David; they would be chastised, and it believed that the Babylonian captivity was the resulting punishment. However, Chafer holds that the covenant would not be annulled.[94] He traces Scripture to portray the promises of this fact in both the Old and New Testaments, and in particular, he draws from Isa 9:6–7, Hos 3:4–5, Luke 1:31–32, Acts 2:25–31, and Rev 22:16.[95] These passages refer in Chafer's thinking to the fact that the reigning king is of the line of David. Chafer interprets these passages literally, and he sees the fulfillment of them in Christ. Chafer gives his summary concerning the Davidic covenant as contained in 2 Sam 7:16:

> In defining Jehovah's new purpose in this present age, which purpose so completely sets aside the essentials of Judaism for a time, the first council of the Church at Jerusalem recognized an order of events which were yet future. There was to be an outcalling of the Church from both Jews and Gentiles, which outcalling has already begun and continues to the present hour. This, in turn, was to be followed and terminated by the return of Christ; and Christ in His return would re-establish the Davidic dynasty.[96]

---

93. Chafer, *Christology*, 321.
94. Chafer, *Christology*, 321.
95. Chafer, *Christology*, 323–29.
96. Chafer, *Christology*, 329.

Both Scofield and Chafer believe that the actual reigning of Christ on the throne is a future event. However, progressive dispensationalists hold that Christ is currently exercising kingship as he is now reigning.

According to classical dispensationalists, there are two major teachings of Christ concerning times future to him, and these are the Olivet Discourse and the Sermon on the Mount. Both Scofield and Chafer believe the former is in reference to the tribulation time on earth. However, both are addressed to Israel. The Olivet Discourse is found in Matt 24 and 25. They articulate that the discourse begins with a description of the tribulation period and concludes with the judgements that will fall upon Israel first and then the nations. The church is interpreted as not present in the Gospel of Matthew; thus, the address is seen to only pertain to Israel:

> The disciples knew nothing of the present Church age (cf. Acts 1:6–7) and therefore could have known nothing about its end. They were living in the Mosaic age, the latter part of which Daniel had predicted would continue for 490 years. He predicted also that the last seven years of that period—Daniel's seventieth week—would be the time of the greatest human upheaval, including the great tribulation, and the presence of the man of sin whom Christ styled "the abomination of desolation, spoken of by Daniel and the prophet" (Matt 24:15; cf. Dan 9:26–27). In other words, the great tribulation and the man of sin belong to the Mosaic age that is past and are wholly unrelated to the present age of the Church. The man of sin will not "stand in the holy place" at the end of the Church age; it is at the end of that age then in effect when the disciples asked the question. The man of sin will stand in the holy place during the tribulation (Matt 24:15; 2 Thess 2:3–4).[97]

Scofield and Chafer both believe that the gospel of the kingdom will be preached during the time of tribulation. The discourse speaks of judgment upon Israel but also the coming in glory of the Lord with the heavenly hosts. It is claimed that this marks the end of the time of tribulation and that the next event to occur on the prophetic calendar is the one-thousand-year reign of Christ.

The Sermon on the Mount is the second important eschatological message Jesus gave. This message is found in Matt 5–7, and classical dispensationalists believe that its primary application is not to the present age of grace but concerns the future kingdom age. Chafer points to the difficulties this passage offered:

97. Chafer, *Christology*, 119–20.

> Apparently, the root difficulty is the failure to recognize what is rightfully a primary and what is rightfully a secondary application of this teaching. When the primary application is given to the Scripture, it is usually a supposition that the Church is the kingdom and therefore passages related to the kingdom are addressed to her. Let it be dogmatically asserted at this point that those who hold such views either have failed to recognize the hopeless, blasting character of the law which this discourse announces and from which the Christian has been saved (Rom 6:14; Gal 5:1), or they have failed to comprehend the present position and perfection in Christ which is the estate of every believer.[98]

Both Scofield and Chafer believe that the sermon itself commences with the proclamation of blessedness to those whose quality of spiritual life meets the specific requirements. There is the promise of the kingdom of heaven itself. During the kingdom reign, there will be a paradox—the humble in spirit will reign. The requirements for the kingdom age are far removed from the previous period, the age of grace. The kingdom requirements are supposedly an extension of the Mosaic law; thus, the keeping of the law is mandatory and not to do so would result in severe consequences in certain situations.

Chafer was concerned about what he believes is a correct interpretation of the Lord's Prayer as contained in Matt 6. He understands the prayer as not for the present age of grace, but belonging by means of primary application to the kingdom age. The Lord's Prayer, he writes,

> At once becomes a most difficult portion of this address for many to release to the kingdom system. In fact, like Matt 5:20 which proclaims the terms of admission into the kingdom for the Jew, the "Lord's prayer" is the divinely prescribed petition for the coming of that kingdom on earth. "Thy kingdom come. Thy will be done on earth as it is in heaven." It is probable that of the many who repeat these words but few have pondered the far-reaching significance. . . . The kingdom will come and the Father's will be done on earth as it is in heaven, but only by virtue of the returning Messiah.[99]

Chafer understands that the passage has legal requirements and is not for those of the present age of grace. He sees the Lord's Prayer as pertaining solely to the kingdom era.

98. Chafer, *Christology*, 97.
99. Chafer, *Christology*, 108.

CLASSICAL DISPENSATIONALISM

All dispensationalists understand that John the Baptist announced with great vigor the coming of the kingdom. They believe that the words of Isa 40:3–5 are prophetic: "A voice cries in the wilderness prepare the way of the Lord; make straight in the desert a highway for our God." Both Scofield and Chafer hold that those who are opposed to chiliasm, have a problem with John the Baptist since they advocate a spiritual kingdom. The reasoning is that if they advocate a spiritual kingdom or no physical kingdom, the message of John the Baptist must be minimized, or even that he was mistaken. Chafer explains,

> It yet remains to be seen that John's ministry served as the consummation of the Old Testament order. Christ said: "For all the prophets and the law prophesied until John" (Matt 11:13), and this is in harmony with the evident fact that John saw the kingdom, which was the subject of the preaching of John, of Christ, and of the disciples until the Messiah was rejected and His kingdom postponed. The kingdom was the national hope and no other objective had been introduced. It was, therefore, most unlikely that some new announced divine program should be the theme of this nation-wide preaching. The confinement of the forerunner in prison (cf. Matt 11:2), the beheading of the same forerunner (Matt 14:10), and the crucifixion of the King Himself serve as final evidence that the kingdom was rejected.[100]

Chafer understands that John's message was not one of salvation by faith in Christ "but rather to a correction of daily life on the part of those who should be thus prepared for their King."[101] The kingdom message, then, had been offered by Christ and the disciples before the death and resurrection of Christ. Israel, both Scofield and Chafer believe, rejected the offer. The offer will again in the future be offered to them, and if accepted, they will be allowed to enter the millennial kingdom itself.

Classical dispensationalists advance the view that only those who have passed through the tribulation period and have been judged as sheep will be allowed to enter the kingdom. Chafer explains,

> Some will have nourished Israel and some will have afflicted them. And of these nations who will have been conquered and broken by the returning King (cf. Ps 2:7–9; Isa 63:1–6; Rev 19:15), some inherit their share—according to much prophecy—in Israel's

---

100. Chafer, *Systematic Theology*, 4:293.
101. Chafer, *Systematic Theology*, 4:294.

kingdom and as designed by the Father from the foundation of the world; those who have afflicted Israel are dismissed into the lake prepared for the devil and his angels. They go to the lake of fire on the ground of their lost estate and as those who are not prepared to enter the kingdom.[102]

Chafer believes that the Scriptures teach there are three classes of nations at the judgment of the nations. The designation, "my brethren," alludes to Israel while the "sheep" refers to those who spiritually belong to God, and the designation "goats" pertains to those who have rejected God. Concerning the very legitimate question of whether the judgment of nations is concerned with the literal nations or individuals, Chafer explains,

> The question inevitably intrudes as to whether this judgment is of nations as entities or of the individual people who comprise the nations. There are arguments advanced in support of each contention. It is likely that to some extent both claims are true. The text declares that the King judges nations as such; yet the kind of service rendered or not rendered—food, shelter, visitation—is such as one individual might supply to another. It should not be overlooked that even now, as never before, the nations are taking sides for or against the Jew. Among those favorable there are individuals who are anti-semitic, and among those unfavorable there are individuals who are semitic in their sympathies. The King alone can and will render a right judgment.
>
> To the nations on the right hand the King declares, "Come ye blessed of my Father, inherit the kingdom prepared for you from the foundations of the world" (Matt 25:34), and for this reason, "For I was thirsty, and ye gave me drink; I was a stranger, and ye took me in; naked and ye clothed me; I was sick, and ye visited me; I was in prison, and ye came unto me" (Matt 24:35–36). Thus a blessing is bestowed which is based on works or *Merit*. This kingdom to which they are invited is not heaven; but rather the earthly kingdom which is promised to Israel.[103]

Gentiles too will enter the kingdom, but only those who have been gracious to Israel. And these individuals will be subservient, Chafer claims, to Israel.[104]

The means by which one enters into a covenantal relationship to God during the millennial age is not conditioned upon grace as in the present

---

102. Chafer, "What Will God Do?," 110.
103. Chafer, "Future of the Gentiles," 155.
104. Chafer, "Future of the Gentiles," 156.

CLASSICAL DISPENSATIONALISM

age of grace. Chafer especially believes this concerning the Beatitudes, which he sees as a kingdom message:

> The intense emphasis on the covenant of meritorious works is obvious in this message; but John did not preach Moses and the prophets. The law and the prophets were *until* John. It is to be concluded that the preaching of John the Baptist was wholly new, and was according to his mission as herald of the King; but that message is legalistic and not gracious. It is a covenant of works and not a covenant of faith.[105]

Chafer, then, articulates that the emphasis during the kingdom will be on conduct and righteousness. He claims that "kingdom teaching extends into the finer details of the law of Moses and never ceases to be the very opposite of the principle of grace."[106] He enumerates three characteristics of the kingdom message: (1) the message is that of the kingdom of heaven or the earthly reign of Christ; (2) two key words in the kingdom are those of "righteousness" and "peace"; (3) the kingdom teachings are based upon a covenant of works.[107] Chafer believes that the kingdom teachings have never been applied to any individual: "The teachings of the kingdom have not been applied to men in all ages; nay, more, they have not been applied to any man. Since they anticipate the binding of Satan, a purified earth, the restoration of Israel, and the personal reign of the King, they cannot be applied until God's appointed time when these accompanying conditions on earth have been brought to pass."[108] The King will reign with an iron hand as iniquity will be rebuked and all forms of sin will be judged in perfect righteousness.[109]

Though the kingdom has not fully come, Chafer emphasizes its existence, he articulates clearly the past and present form of the kingdom:

> The kingdom of heaven, since it embraces the rule of God in the earth, is subject to various modes of manifestation in Israel's history and that of the world. (1) The theocracy of the Old Testament was a form of divine rule in the earth, and hence an aspect of the kingdom of heaven. (2) The covenant with David is the kingdom of heaven in covenant form. (3) Prophecy concerning the scope and character of the kingdom of heaven is that rule in prophetic form.

---

105. Chafer, *Systematic Theology*, 4:214–15.
106. Chafer, *Christology*, 344.
107. Chafer, *Systematic Theology*, 4:215–16.
108. Chafer, *Systematic Theology*, 4:207.
109. Chafer, *Systematic Theology*, 4:207.

> (4) The announcing of that kingdom by John the Baptist (Matt 3:1–2), by Christ (Matt 4:17), and by His disciples (Matt 10:5–7) was the kingdom of heaven offered. (5) The subsequent rejection and postponement of the kingdom of heaven became a phase of that kingdom. (6) The present age, though so wholly without comparison with that which went before or with that which follows, does, nevertheless, include a form of divine rule on earth. The purpose of the present age is the realization of those features which are styled *mysteries*, that is, hitherto unrevealed divine purposes. God is now ruling in the earth to the extent that He accomplishes all that is embraced in those mysteries. This age thus becomes the kingdom of heaven in its mystery form (cf. Matt 13:11). Certain other truths obtain at the same time, namely, that government is committed to Gentiles until their times are fulfilled (Luke 21:24), that Satan exercises a large authority over the kingdoms of this world (Matt 4:8–9; Luke 4:5–7), that the "powers that be" are ordained of God (Rom 13:1). In the last analysis, there is nothing in the realm of authority which is outside the permissive will of God. (7) The final form of the kingdom of heaven is that which will yet be set up in its fullest manifestation in the earth and in compliance with all that God has spoken. What that final form is to be is disclosed in the predictions, covenants, and promises of God.[110]

Thus, Chafer constructs an understanding of the kingdom with elements of both the Old and New Testaments.

There are at least five characteristics of the kingdom: (1) the kingdom will be theocratic; (2) the kingdom will be heavenly in character; (3) it will be over regathered and converted Israel; (4) the kingdom will be established by the returning King; and (5) the reign will be spiritual.[111] In summary, it can be said that the King will reign over his people and his authority will be unquestioned. Satan, according to Chafer, will be bound at the beginning of the millennial reign; therefore, he cannot entice the saints. Chafer comments, "The scriptures abundantly testify that, while there will be far less occasion to sin, for the sufficient reason that Satan is then bound and in a pit and the glorious King is on His throne, there will be need of immediate execution of judgment and justice in the earth, and even the King shall rule, of necessity, with a 'rod of iron.'"[112] Chafer believes there will be a limited amount of evil manifested in the millennium, but it will be

110. Chafer, *Systematic Theology*, 4:326–27.
111. Chafer, *Christology*, 334–40.
112. Chafer, *Christology*, 346.

judged quickly.[113] It must be kept in mind that Chafer holds to three sources of sin: Satan, the world system or the *cosmos*, and the flesh. The latter is the only one of the three that will be present during the millennial period, but the reality of the lust of the flesh is ever pervasive, and this is why the Lord must rule with an iron hand, according to Chafer.

He did not go into detail about what the condition of the environment will be during the millennial reign of Christ. He did, however, quote Isa 11:6–9, which refers to the subduing of the animal kingdom. If interpreted literally, Isa 55:12–13 speaks of the absence of thorns and briars. Micah 4:3 anticipates a time when the nations will no longer be at war. The promise of God's total forgiveness of the sins of Israel is promised in Jer 31:33–34. The millennium is depicted as a time of peace.

Both Scofield and Chafer believe that the millennium, the literal thousand-year reign of Christ, will close with specific and cataclysmic events, just as did the age of law with the death of Christ and as the age of grace will with the translation of the living saints. Chafer argues that there are seven events that will mark the transition from the literal, earthly kingdom age to the eternal estate:

> There are seven stupendous events which mark the transition to be wrought between the kingdom age and eternity to come: (1) the release of Satan from the abyss, (2) the revolt on earth with judgments upon Satan and his armies, (3) the passing of the old heaven and the old earth, (4) the great white throne judgment, (5) creation of a new heaven and a new earth, (6) the descent of the bridal city from God out of heaven, and (7) the surrender of the mediatorial aspect of Christ's reign and adjustment to the eternal state following immediately.[114]

The release of Satan, both Scofield and Chafer articulate, occurs at the end of the kingdom age; Chafer especially bases his interpretation for this event upon Rev 19:7–8. Satan, then, is the catalyst behind a final battle on earth that Chafer terms "Gog and Magog." He writes vividly concerning the conduct of this fallen angel:

> Thus, it is intimated that Satan is ever deceiving the nations, excepting for the period of his binding and until his final dismissal to the lake of fire. Much like the unceasing pressure of the sin nature on the individual's life is the influence of Satan upon the mass of

---

113. Chafer, *Systematic Theology*, 7:238.
114. Chafer, *Christology*, 359–60.

humanity, inciting to war, greed, self-manifestations, and impious conduct. What even a day's release of the individual from the pressure of the sin nature would mean in actual experience or a day's release for humanity from the deceptions of Satan cannot be imagined; but humanity, whether released from the sin nature or not, will be released from the Satanic deceptions during the kingdom reign of Christ upon the earth. It will be noted that the last army ever to be assembled will be drawn from the four quarters of the earth and "Gog and Magog," which designation is perhaps more a reference to the event in question rather than to any locality or specific peoples.[115]

Chafer looks to Rev 20 to substantiate the fact that the present order of the earth and heavens will pass. The final resurrection and the Great White Throne Judgment are events concerned with the same class of individuals, those who are unregenerate. According to Rev 21:1, Chafer believes that a new heaven and earth will be created:

> It may yet be observed that, in the picture of the new earth, the all-important feature is that "the tabernacle of God" will be with men. Such a situation has not obtained before. Earth has been the sphere of sin and corruption unsuited to the presence of God; but it will then be as holy as heaven, and in the new earth He will delight to dwell among men and to be their God. The term *men* is evidently in contradistinction to the Biblical term *saints*. Heaven will be, as now, the abode of the saints, while earth will be the abode of men.... In the eternal new heaven and earth righteousness shall *dwell*.[116]

Chafer espouses that the heavenly city will come into view for those who are upon the earth. He finds his biblical support for the city from Rev 21. Chafer believes "that it [the city] is of pure gold [and] is wholly within the creative power of God and an intimation may be found here respecting the glory of the new heaven and the new earth. The city descends from heaven and is therefore to be considered, to some degree, as something apart from heaven. It is named the Bride of Christ.... It becomes a cosmopolitan center."[117]

Chafer calls attention to the debate concerning the mediatorial role of Christ in the future. It has been interpreted by some that Christ will withdraw as King at the end of the thousand-year reign, according to 1 Cor

---

115. Chafer, *Christology*, 361.
116. Chafer, *Christology*, 366.
117. Chafer, *Christology*, 367.

15:24–28. However, Chafer holds that there are literally scores of passages that state the opposite; he will in the future reign on the throne of David, both Scofield and Chafer claim. Such biblical passages include 2 Sam 7:16; Ps 89:3–4, 34–37; Heb 1:8; Jer 33:14–17, 20–21; and Ezek 37:24–28. Chafer believes that he answered the problem by stating that Christ will still reign but as he always has, under the rule and authority of the Father. The authority for Christ's kingship is an outgrowth of his deity. "He will, as so fully assured elsewhere, reign on the throne of David forever."[118]

Influence of Classical Dispensationalism

Classical dispensationalism as seen in the writings of both Scofield and Chafer has waned over the past few years. Some see classical dispensationalism as outmoded and divisive, especially those who hold more of a Reformed view of theology. Chafer was theologically Reformed, though of course, he held a modified view since Calvinistic theology would not embrace dispensationalism; however, he embraces the essential tenets of the Reformed faith including a strong emphasis on the sovereignty of God, the divinity of Christ, the authority of the Scriptures, justification by faith, and the belief in a literal second coming of Christ. Concerning Chafer's influence, Grudem writes,

> While Chafer's position continues to have influence in some dispensational circles, and certainly in more popular preaching, a number of leaders among more recent dispensationalists have not followed Chafer in many of these points. Several current dispensational theologians, such as Robert Saucy, Craig Blaising, and Darrell Bock, refer to themselves as "progressive dispensationalists," and they have gained a wide following. They *would not see the church as a parenthesis* in God's plan but as the first step toward the establishment of the kingdom of God. On a progressive dispensational view, *God does not have two separate purposes for Israel and the church*, but a single purpose—the establishment of the kingdom of God—in which Israel and the church will both share. Progressive dispensationalists would see *no distinction between Israel and the church in the future eternal state*, for all will be part of one people of God. Moreover, they would hold that the church will reign with Christ *in glorified bodies on earth during the millennium*. However, there is still a difference between progressive

---

118. Chafer, *Christology*, 374.

dispensationalists and the rest of evangelicalism on one point: they would say that *the Old Testament prophecies concerning Israel will still be fulfilled in the millennium by ethnic Jewish people* who will believe in Christ and live in the land of Israel as a "model nation" for all nations to see and learn from. Therefore they would not say that the church is the "new Israel" or that all the Old Testament prophecies about Israel will yet be fulfilled in the church, for these prophecies will yet be fulfilled in ethnic Israel.[119]

The Scofield and Chafer interpretation, then, is viewed as essentially antiquated by progressive dispensationalists, though certainly this view impacted evangelicalism for many decades. Their views were embraced by many theological seminaries, including Talbot Theological Seminary, Dallas Theological Seminary, and Moody Bible Institute—all fully accredited schools of theology that have been in existence for over one hundred years. Such schools promoted an academic study of classical dispensationalism but have recently embraced overall the progressive approach—especially in eschatology.

The classical dispensational method influenced the Bible conference movements, especially in the United States and Canada, such as Northfield Bible Conferences in Northfield, Massachusetts, Niagara Bible Conferences in Niagara-on-the Lake, Ontario, and America's Keswick in Whiting, New Jersey. These were seen as locations of spiritual renewal for many, especially in the late nineteen and early twentieth centuries; America's Keswick continues to have a vibrant ministry.

Biblical themes were preached and taught and classical dispensationalism was the core message presented. James Hall Brooks (1830–97), a Presbyterian minister who attended Princeton Theological Seminary, hosted John Nelson Darby at his church. Brookes was the chairperson of the Niagara Bible Conference, and he is credited with introducing C. I. Scofield to dispensationalism. Brookes was the author of *Maranatha*, a book that popularized dispensationalism during his time.

Adoniram Judson Gordon (1836–95) was another well-known leader in the Bible conference movement who promoted dispensationalism. He worked closely with D. L. Moody and is believed to have influenced Moody's dispensational theological position.

Arno C. Gaebelein (1861–1945), born in Germany, and came to the United States as a young person. He was the editor of *Our Hope* magazine.

---

119. Grudem, *Systematic Theology*, 860 (emphasis original).

Timothy Weber writes concerning Gaebelein that he "acquired such an expertise in the Talmud and other rabbinic literature and spoke such flawless Yiddish that he often had a difficult time convincing many of his audience that he was not a Jew trying to pass as a Gentile."[120] Gaebelein promoted dispensationalism primary through the *Our Hope* publication.

William E. Blackstone (1841–1935) lived in Chicago and was the author of the well-known book *Jesus is Coming*, published in 1878. Many claim that he was one of the major fathers of the Zionist movement even though he was a Christian. Blackstone promoted dispensationalism primary through his writings.

Classical dispensationalism, then, continues to have an influence especially with those outside of an academic milieu and of an older generation. There has been some resistance on the part of some scholarship to accept progressive dispensationalism either for theological reasons or due to the opinion that the Darby-Scofield-Chafer tradition is the standard and should not be altered. An example of this is Charles Ryrie's opinion:

> One expects that there will be further revisions and changes in progressive dispensationalism as time passes. Where it will all lead and whether or not it will be understood and received by those who have embraced normative dispensationalism, no one knows. But already progressive dispensationalism certainly appears to be more than a development within normative dispensational teaching. Some so-called developments are too radical not to be called changes.
>
> Little wonder that some nondispensational critics of progressive dispensationalism see it as having already changed to covenant premillennialism or, at least clearly pointing to that view. . . . Walter A. Elwell thinks that progressive dispensationalism "will be warmly received by nondispensationalists" and concludes that "the newer dispensationalism looks so much like nondispensationalist premillennialism that one struggles to see any real differences." And more, Poythress predicts that the progressives position "is inherently unstable. I do not think that they will find it possible in the long run to create a safe haven theologically between classic dispensationalism and covenantal premillennialism. The forces that their own observations have set in motion will most likely lead to a covenantal premillennialism after the pattern of George E. Ladd."[121]

---

120. Weber, *Shadow of the Second Coming*, 144.

121. Ryrie, *Dispensationalism*, 209–10, quoting Elwell, "Third Kind," 28; and

Ryrie's critique includes more interesting observations:

> Actually the label "progressive dispensationalism" was introduced at the 1991 meeting [of the Evangelical Theological Society in Atlanta, Georgia], since "significant revisions in dispensationalism had taken place by that time. Darrell L. Bock of Dallas Theological Seminary and Craig A. Blaising, formerly a professor of Systematic Theology at Dallas, have been in the forefront of the movement, along with Robert L. Saucy (Systematic Theology) of Talbot Theological Seminary....
>
> In the overall historical picture of dispensational theology, this new movement inaugurates an era clearly distinguished from previous eras of dispensational thought. The initial period started with J. N. Darby and continued through the publication of L. S. Chafer's *Systematic Theology* in 1948. Progressives label this the classical period. (I personally think it makes better sense to divide the early/Darby era from the Scofield/Chafer period.) The second or third era extends from the 1950s almost to the 1990s and includes the writings of Alva McClain, John Walvoord, J. Dwight Pentecost, and myself. This was first called by progressives the essentialist period (from my listing of the essentials—the *sine qua non*—of dispensationalism), but more recently it has been changed to the revised period. The third (or fourth) present period differs from the previous ones because it includes "a number of modifications" and "sufficient revisions."[122]

For certain theologians, classical dispensationalism has somewhat of a short life span, about 150 years, but its influence in many theological circles was enormous as all the major doctrines were interpreted considering this particular theological stance. Even though it has been argued that dispensationalism has its genesis in Reformed theology, historically the rift between classical dispensationalism and Reformed theology has been at times most controversial and even bitter. The new movement, progressive dispensationalism, appears to be an attempt at some reconciliation between the two theological interpretations.

Classical dispensational heavily influenced many Protestant denominations in the United States and other countries through preaching, teaching, literature, and graduates of various colleges, universities, and theological seminaries. However, the variety of hermeneutical interpretations within dispensationalism, especially that of the classical position,

---

Poythress, *Understanding Dispensationalists*, 137.

122. Ryrie, *Dispensationalism*, 190.

promotes a wide variety of conclusions within this theological position; thus, the new movement of progressive dispensationalism appears to be a natural progression of classical dispensationalism.

Conclusion

Though John N. Darby is usually cited as the father of dispensationalism, some argue that the foundational teachings go back many centuries as seen in the writings of Justin Martyr and Tertullian. Arnold Ehlert argues that the writings of both the writings of both John Edwards and the later theologian, Jonathan Edwards, contain in outline form a semblance of dispensational divisions of biblical history.

The interpretation of the biblical word "kingdom" is certainly a key component for establishing an eschatological understanding of how history will unfold. Augustine is typically credited with the amillennial understanding, which posits the kingdom in the present experience of the church. This view is perhaps the dominant position within Christianity historically and currently.

Daniel Whitby is credited by many to be the father of postmillennialism which has had somewhat of a sporadic history as one of the eschatological positions. Of the three major views of how history and time will continue, postmillennialism is the most positive in its view of the kingdom, arguing that world conditions will gradually continue to improve and then the second coming of Christ will occur. Virkler, however argues, "Postmillennialism—the view that the church will eventually win the world for Christ and usher in the millennium—rapidly lost popularity during the first half of the twentieth century. The carnage of the world wars was a grim reminder to most postmillennialists that the world was *not* being won for Christ. Hence the majority of evangelical Christians today identify themselves as either premillennialists or amillennialists."[123] Weber argues that postmillennialism did not entirely disappear but morphed into other forms, such as Albrecht Ritschl's view that the kingdom of God is ethical rather than eschatological. Weber believes that those who promoted the American social gospel retained much of the postmillennial agenda without using the Old Testament biblical passages so common in premillennialism,

---

123. Virkler and Ayayo, *Hermeneutics*, 178–79.

and that in the twentieth century remnants of postmillennialism appeared in the Progressive movement, New Deal, and the civil rights movement.[124]

Historically, there have been many theologians who have identified as classical dispensationalists, notably C. I. Scofield and Lewis Sperry Chafer. The former promoted dispensational teachings primarily through his copious notes as contained in *The Scofield Reference Bible* while the latter by means of his eight-volume *Systematic Theology*, which was a standard text in some seminaries.

Virkler gives insight into how classical dispensationalism has morphed into its current status:

> In 1965 Charles Ryrie wrote *Dispensationalism Today*, and two years later the *New Scofield Reference Bible* was published. Both books modified a number of teachings of earlier dispensationalism. Some theologians have referred to Ryrie's theory as "essentialist dispensationalism" since it identified certain essential features that he believed distinguished dispensationalism from covenant theology.
>
> From the 1990s to the present the dispensational movement has been referred to as "postessentialist" or "progressive" dispensationalism. It is considered post-essential because the heterogeneity among both dispensational and covenantal theologians has made it increasingly difficult to identify essential differences that consistently differentiate one group from the other.[125]

George Eldon Ladd argues that the church during her first three hundred years understood eschatology in terms of premillennialism; this view is sometime referred to as "historical premillennialism." Ladd promotes a view he termed, "already but not yet," meaning he believes that the kingdom has already been initiated but is not yet in all its fullness.[126] However, Weber gives insight into how millennialism is understood in most Christian groupings:

> In the twenty-first century, most Roman Catholics, Orthodox, and Protestants do not think about the future in millennialist terms. Traditionalists in all three groups, however, retain belief in a historical Antichrist, the Parousia, the resurrection of the dead, and the last judgment within some version of Augustinian amillennialism. Following the Enlightenment, more progressive Christians have reinterpreted these biblical concepts in other ways. In the

124. Weber, "Millennialism," 378.
125. Weber, "Millennialism," 128.
126. Ladd, *Crucial Questions*, 21–39.

mid-twentieth century, R. Bultmann argued that it is necessary to "demythologize" apocalyptic texts so they could be appreciated in existentialist, rather than in cosmological or historical, terms. Another popular option was C. H. Dodd's realized eschatology, which shifted focus to the present, not the future, since Jesus had already established the kingdom of God. In more recent decades, J. Moltmann and W. Pannenberg promoted a "theology of hope," which revived notions of realistic eschatology by considering the historical Parousia and the establishment of God's kingdom on earth without resorting to apocalyptic excesses.[127]

---

127. Weber, "Millennialism," 379.

Chapter Two

Progressive Dispensationalism

Origin of Progressive Dispensationalism

PROGRESSIVE DISPENSATIONALISM IS VIEWED—ESPECIALLY by those who hold to classical dispensationalism—as having gone too far and, in a sense, those who hold to this theological persuasion are seen as having conceded to the proponents of Reformed theology. Classical dispensationalists have cited arguments such as misinterpretation of texts, disrespect of previous theologians, and a rejection of a correct hermeneutical method of interpretation.

Dispensationalism has a long history in the church, close to two-hundred years, and is ingrained in many theological circles especially in Great Britain and the United States. Of course, there have been a myriad of critics of dispensationalism; perhaps the harshest have been from those who hold to a Reformed theological persuasion, which particular stance embraces amillennialism and not any form of premillennialism. Classical dispensationalism had a strong influence on the Bible conference movement and was also present in several theological seminaries, thus influencing vast numbers of those who would enter the ministry either as pastors or professors in various theological disciplines.

Progressive dispensationalism was a gargantuan shift in dispensational theology; as it goes against the established interpretation of key issues such as the Davidic covenant's application and the kingdom reign of

Christ, many who held to the classical dispensational viewed the new position as almost quasi-heretical. Some of this dissention was caused by the fact that many who held to the classical dispensational did not want their long-standing position to be viewed as antiquated or even unscriptural. The fear on the part of many was that the long-held position, which was embraced by many respected past theologians, would be seen as illogical and indebted to a wrong hermeneutical method; thus, the resistance on the part of the classical theologians to the progressive dispensationalists' position resulted in a heated controversy.

Inherent within classical dispensationalism is a revising ethos—that is, as a theological position, dispensationalism has always been controversial. To detractors, dispensationalism seems to even be on the level of a cult, a belief system seemingly outside of historic Christianity. Essentially, both amillennialism, which is the majority view in Christianity, and postmillennialism have a similar view concerning eschatology. Both hold to the position that there will be in the future a second coming of Christ and then a judgment to determine the destiny of persons. However, classical dispensationalism, especially, is quite detailed in comparison to either an amillennial or postmillennial stance. It employs more of a literal hermeneutic concerning how to interpret especially Old Testament passages. Symbolic interpretation is not ignored but is relegated to a level of secondary importance in comparison to a historical-grammatical interpretation. Classical dispensationalism, for example, believes that the Old Testament book of Daniel—in particular, chapter 9—is to be interpreted as a yet future event and that the seventieth week of Daniel is a period of seven years of tribulation on earth, especially for the nation of Israel. There is a belief in a literal antichrist who will sway many to follow his political and religious agendas; there will be a last battle, usually referred to as Armageddon; and the saints will be "raptured" or taken up. There are a variety of interpretations of when this will take place—ranging from before the tribulation begins, to the midpoint of the tribulation, or at the conclusion of the period of seven years.

Contemporary dispensationalists, who were young in the 1980s and 1990s, began to question many of the premises of classical dispensationalism. Some of these issues revolved around the basic hermeneutics of the older version of dispensationalism, which came to be seen as somewhat simplistic and perhaps too literal in the interpretation of select biblical passages. The rigid distinction between Israel and the church also became a matter of debate. The long-standing contention between dispensationalists and those of the Reformed faith was almost a heated family discussion since many argued that dispensationalism had its roots in Reformed theology. There were also some more subtle matters, including the fact that the progressive dispensationalists were seen as having stronger academic credentials since those who founded the new perspective all had post-graduate theological degrees from leading universities. The debate between both classical dispensationalism and progressive dispensationalism will continue. The former believe that the latter have conceded too much to Reformed theology and have also engaged in a less than literal hermeneutic, especially pertaining to what are believed to be significant prophetic passages.

Rather than having its genesis in one theologian and then several successors such as Darby, Scofield, and Chafer, progressive dispensationalism began as various scholars shared common concerns and called for a remodeling of the older scheme of dispensationalism. These persons held academic positions at recognized schools of theology, had years of experience as academicians, and were published authors. The three that will be examined are professors of theology, two at Dallas Theological Seminary and one at Talbot Theological Seminary. Both seminaries are dispensational and are fully accredited with the Association of Theological Schools in the United States and Canada.

Ryrie claims that the new movement is "an era clearly distinguished from previous eras of dispensational thought."[1] It is necessary, then, to discuss what sets progressive dispensationalism apart from the previous interpretation, or classical dispensationalism.

Key Theologians

Classical dispensationalism had a long history of diverse theologians. Some of them were highly educated such as William Henry Griffith Thomas (1861–1924) who had a DD from Christ College, Oxford, and served as principal of Wycliffe College, Oxford, from 1905–1910. He also taught at Wycliffe College in Toronto, Ontario, from 1910–20. He was a theologically conservative Anglican. Thomas was the author of several works including *The Principles of Theology*, a systematic theology patterned after the Thirty-Nine Articles of the Anglican Communion. He was a classical

---

1. Ryrie, *Dispensationalism*, 190.

dispensationalist and was a popular speaker and lecturer. He and Lewis Sperry Chafer cofounded Dallas Theological Seminary in 1924.

Classical dispensationalism also had many well-known pastors. One such person was Donald Grey Barnhouse (1895–1960), the pastor of Tenth Street Presbyterian Church in Philadelphia, Pennsylvania. Barnhouse attended both the University of Chicago and Princeton Theological Seminary. He was well-known for both his preaching and teaching ministry as well as the author of many books. Barnhouse's book on Romans was especially well received. As a dispensationalist in a Reformed denomination, Presbyterian Church USA, he was at times at odds with the standard doctrine of the denomination, which did not accept dispensationalism.

R. A. Torrey (1856–1928) had a significant influence upon Barnhouse and introduced him to dispensationalism. Torrey was a graduate of both Yale College and Yale Divinity School. He was heavily involved in both academia and evangelistic ministry.

In more recent years, one of the better-known classical dispensationalists was Charles Caldwell Ryrie (1925–2016). Ryrie received his PhD from Edinburgh University in Scotland; he then taught at Dallas Theological Seminary for thirty years. The author of many books, perhaps his best-known works are the *NIV Ryrie Study Bible* and *Dispensationalism*. Ryrie continued to hold to classical dispensationalism, and his primary work on the subject has been a major reference for those who oppose progressive dispensationalism. Virkler writes the following concerning Ryrie's influence:

> In 1965 Charles Ryrie wrote *Dispensationalism Today*, and two years later the *New Scofield Reference Bible* was published. Both books modified a number of teachings of earlier dispensationalism. Some theologians have referred to Ryrie's theory as "essentialist dispensationalism" since it identified certain features that he believed distinguished dispensationalism from covenant theology.
>
> From the 1990s to the present the dispensational movement has been referred to as "postessentialist" or "progressive" dispensationalism. It is considered postessentialist because the heterogeneity among both dispensational and covenant theologians has made it increasingly difficult to identify essential differences that consistently differentiate one group from the other.[2]

---

2. Virkler and Ayayo, *Hermeneutics*, 128.

There are many others who could be cited, both prominent pastors and theologians; however, such a survey is not necessary. Many were well-known theologians, authors, and pastors.

Because the history of progressive dispensationalism is quite brief in comparison to classical dispensationalism, there are fewer key representatives of this position. Three are examined here.

Robert L. Saucy (1930–2010) was a professor at Talbot School of Theology. He was one of three scholars who worked on the *New American Standard Bible* in 1971 and the revision done in 1995. Saucy went beyond classical dispensationalism toward a more Reformed view of the church and Israel. He writes,

> The biblical teaching on "the people of God" provides the fundamental outline of the relationship of Israel and the church. In the final sense it is perhaps best to say that "the people of God" are one people because all will be related to him through the same covenant salvation. But this fundamental unity in relation to God through Christ does not remove Israel's distinction as a special nation called of God for a unique ministry in the world as a nation among nations. Nor does it define the totality of the people of God as "Israel," requiring that the church is somehow a "new Israel."[3]

Ryrie, a classical dispensationalist, strongly disagreed with Saucy and was critical of Saucy's understanding that the church is inherent in the view of "the people of God," having its origins with the nation of Israel.[4] Of course, classical dispensationalism holds that the church did not begin until after the ascension of Christ and the beginning is recorded in the first chapters of the book of Acts, on the day of Pentecost. This is a remarkable change on the part of Saucy who previously had written a book entitled *The Church in God's Program* (1972) which is a classical dispensational interpretation of the origins of the church. The work was used as a seminary text by many schools for several years; thus, when Saucy revised his understanding of the genesis of the church, many took notice since he is viewed as an authority concerning the classical view of the origins of the church.

Craig Blaising is one of the major persons involved in the reinterpretation of significant areas within dispensationalism. Trained in classical dispensationalism, he completed his PhD at Aberdeen University in Scotland. Recognized as an authority in patristics, Blaising also has a ThD

---

3. Saucy, *Progressive Dispensationalism*, 190.
4. Ryrie, *Dispensationalism*, 153–54.

from Dallas Theological Seminary, served on the faculty as professor of systematic theology, and was also a professor and served as associate vice president of doctoral studies at Southern Baptist Theological Seminary in Louisville, Kentucky.

Darrell Bock is the third person, alongside both Saucy and Blaising, who has garnered both the interest and displeasure of many. Bock received his PhD from Aberdeen University in Scotland and has been a professor of New Testament at Dallas Theological Seminary for several decades. Both he and Blaising coauthored the book *Progressive Dispensationalism* (1993). Bock was also a Humboldt Scholar at Tübingen University for multiple years.

Concerning the impact of Saucy, Blaising, and Bock, Grudem states,

> While Chafer's position continues to have influence in some dispensational circles, and certainly in more popular preaching, a number of leaders among more recent dispensationalists have not followed Chafer in many of these points. Several current dispensational theologians, such as Robert Saucy, Craig Blaising, and Darrell Bock, refer to themselves as "progressive dispensationalists," and they have gained a wide following. They *would not see the church as a parenthesis* in God's plan but as the first step toward the establishment of the kingdom of God. On a progressive dispensational view, *God does not have two separate purposes for Israel and the church*, but a single purpose—in which Israel and the church will both share. Progressive Dispensationalists would see *no distinction between Israel and the church in the future eternal state*, for all will be part of the people of God. Moreover, they would hold that the church will reign with Christ in *glorified bodies on earth during the millennium*. However, there is still a difference between progressive dispensationalists and the rest of evangelicalism on one point: they would say that *Old Testament prophecies concerning Israel will still be fulfilled in the millennium by ethic Jewish people* who will believe in Christ and live in the land of Israel as a "model nation" for all nations to see and learn from. Therefore, they would not say that the church is a "new Israel" or that all the Old Testament prophecies about Israel will be fulfilled in the church, for these prophecies will yet be fulfilled in ethnic Israel.[5]

There are many distinctions between classical dispensationalism and progressive dispensationalism. These significant differences will be discussed.

---

5. Grudem, *Systematic Theology*, 860 (emphasis original).

The Issues

To state the obvious, progressive dispensationalism is still considered to be dispensationalism; however, some accuse the newly-revised position to be a major aberration. Ryrie states,

> One expects that there will be further revisions and changes in progressive dispensationalism as time passes. Where it will all lead and whether or not it will be understood and received by those who have embraced normative dispensationalism, no one knows. But already progressive dispensationalism certainly appears to be more than a development within normative dispensational teaching. Some so-called developments are too radical not to be called changes.[6]

So, the lines have been drawn between the classical and progressive dispensationalists. This change seems to be almost predictable since many of the key dispensationalists were steeped heavily in Reformed theology and not Arminian theology; therefore, issues of God's sovereignty, the limits of the human will, the authority of Scripture, the divinity of Christ, the reality of sin, the prophetic nature of both the New and Old Testaments, and the second coming as a literal event were all taken seriously. Theologians such as Augustine, Calvin, many of the Reformers, Jonathan Edwards, and Machen all are taken seriously, even though they were not dispensationalists, by either classical and progressive dispensationalist standards. Interestingly, Ryrie claims the following:

> Many who formerly had been associated with the normative dispensational camp have embraced the revised view, especially in academia. Much of the dialog has been between progressives and covenant theologians, who have openly expressed pleasure that progressives have moved away from normative dispensationalism, though covenant theologians clearly have not moved from the tenets of their position. . . . In an attempt to justify their movement away from normative dispensationalism, progressives have pointed to differences in some interpretations among dispensationalists. They conclude that, if normatives can do it, their revisions are justified also. However, the crucial consideration is not that there are some differences, but what those differences are. Are they minor or major? In general, differences in interpretations and emphases among normative dispensationalists do not change

---

6. Ryrie, *Dispensationalism*, 209.

the overall system of dispensationalism, whereas the differences advanced by progressive dispensationalists do form a new and revised system that some (both dispensationalists and nondispensationalists) believe is not dispensationalism anymore.[7]

Poythress argues that progressive dispensationalism is actually in line with covenantal premillennialism and "is inherently unstable. I do not think that they will find it possible in the long run to create a safe haven theologically between classic dispensationalism and covenantal premillennialism. The forces that their own observations have set in motion will most likely lead to covenantal premillennialism after the pattern of George E. Ladd."[8]

There are many areas of difference and dispute between classical and progressive dispensationalists; however, there are four that are central, and these will be discussed. They are as follows: the understanding of the Davidic covenant, the new covenant, the church and Israel, and the method of interpretation. Each one of these has vastly different interpretations, which only to some seem not to be major reinterpretations; however, to most the revisions seem to move progressive dispensationalism out of the category of dispensationalism, either toward a covenantal position or even within this theological stance. Those who see the revisions as a new interpretation view them almost as a concession to covenant theology and an aberration of classical dispensationalism.

Dispensationalism has historically placed a great emphasis on the covenants in the Old Testament. They have seen them as unifying themes not only in the Old Testament but also in the New Testament. With the heavy emphasis upon an historical-grammatical hermeneutic, those who hold to classical dispensationalism believe more in the literal fulfillment of each one of these and overall see them as unconditional—that is, there are no conditions on the part of God's people, and the covenants will be fulfilled according to God's perfect will. Of course, the emphasis on the covenants and their fulfillment is connected to the classical dispensational view of the prophetic nature of both the Old and New Testaments; the view is that if interpreted literally and according to standard grammatical rules, the conclusion will be that the selected passages that are seen to be prophetic will be fulfilled. Of course, classical dispensationalists understand that the majority of these passages have already been fulfilled—for example, in the Assyrian or the Babylonian captivities; they would interpret Isa 53,

---

7. Ryrie, *Dispensationalism*, 190–91.
8. Poythress, *Understanding Dispensationalists*, 137.

for example, as alluding to the Messiah who has already come for the first advent, while other passages would pertain to the second advent of Christ.

Interpretations

Classical dispensationalists believe that the Davidic covenant as contained in 2 Sam 7:4–16 is prophetic, and Chafer, for example, articulates that this covenant is not conditional but is unconditional—that is, the covenant will be fulfilled. He along with many other classical dispensationalists claim that David was promised a perpetual royal lineage that would be both a throne and a literal earthly kingdom. The understanding is that all of these promises are set in time; thus, they will ultimately be fulfilled. Chafer writes,

> From the day that the covenant was made and confirmed by Jehovah's oath (Acts 2:30) to the birth of Christ, David did not lack for a son to sit on his throne (Jer. 33:21), and Christ the Eternal Son of God and Son of David, being the rightful heir to that throne and the One who will yet sit on that throne (Luke 1:31–33), completes the fulfillment of this promise to David that a Son would sit on the throne forever.[9]

This promise by God to David, it is believed, would be ultimately fulfilled with the coming of the Messiah after his second coming. After this event, the Messiah, Jesus, will literally assume his position on the throne and will reign over a literal, earthly kingdom for a period of one thousand years—this is the period of time referred to as the millennial reign of Christ. Poythress, a covenant theologian, gives some insight concerning the controversy:

> Doubtless dispensationalists would still not be satisfied with my view. What they have in mind is a *millennial* kingdom for Israel, a kingdom on *this* old earth, not the new earth. Many (but not all) of them think that a radical distinction must be made at this point, because they still envision the new earth of the consummation as entirely other than and unrelated to this present earth. Only the millennial earth remains in substantial continuity with this present earth. But here the miscommunication is a real danger. Their "new earth" is not the same as my new earth. Instead, my new earth is practically indistinguishable from their millennial earth. In fact, I think that it is even better than they imagine. All evil is gone.[10]

---

9. Chafer, *Major Themes*, 108–9.
10. Poythress, *Understanding Dispensationalists*, 133.

Chafer's view seemingly corresponds to Poythress's depiction. Chafer believes that the Davidic covenant concerns an actual earthly throne and is related to a people whose expectation is earthly. He does not believe that this is a heavenly throne nor that the earthly reign will merge into a spiritual one. He claims that the reign will be established on earth when the Lord returns for a second time; he bases his conclusion upon Matt 25:31–32 and Luke 1:31–33.

The major issue of disagreement between the classical dispensationalists and the progressive dispensationalists is whether Jesus is currently reigning as king on the throne. The classical dispensationalists have held historically that he is not in the present age, but that he will be in the coming one-thousand-year reign on earth. Rather than discuss the extended arguments of classical dispensationalists about when the actual reign of Christ will occur, Blaising and Bock offer a summary of the issue:

> In controversies between covenantalists and dispensationalists . . . objections have been raised against both present and future fulfillments of the Davidic promise. Some dispensationalists object to interpreting Christ's past and present relationship with the Father as well as His present session in terms of the Davidic covenant. They believe that Davidic covenant blessings will only and completely be fulfilled at Christ's return when he rules over Israel and all nations. Some covenantists object to the belief that there will be a future fulfillment of national-political aspects of the Davidic covenant when Christ returns to the earth. They believe that the Davidic promise is completely fulfilled in Jesus' present session.[11]

Ryrie argues that the progressive dispensationalists are actually very close to the covenantal or Reformed tradition in the understanding of the fulfillment of the Davidic covenant. He states, "Little wonder that some dispensational critics of progressive dispensationalism see it as having already changed to covenant premillennialism or, at least, clearly leading to that view."[12]

Ryrie also adds a helpful discussion to understand the dispensationalist's view of the origin of covenant theology. He summarizes the history of the genesis of covenant theology, writing,

> To sum up: Covenant theology is a post-Reformation development in doctrine. It began as a reaction to extreme Calvinism but

11. Blaising and Bock, *Progressive Dispensationalism*, 181.
12. Ryrie, *Dispensationalism*, 209.

> soon became the handmaid of Calvinism. The covenant statement in the Westminster Confession is undeveloped; it was Cocceius who developed the idea and Witsius who made it a governing category of scriptural interpretation. Covenant theology as taught today is a development from both the theology of the Reformers (who did not teach a covenant scheme at all) and the teachings of Cocceius and the Westminster Confession. Covenant theology is not the theology of the Reformers; neither is covenant theology today the same as it was when originally introduced. Covenant theology is a refinement—and the refining did not antedate Darby by many years. Covenant theology cannot claim much more antiquity than dispensationalism, and in its present form it is considerably refined. If lack of antiquity is detrimental and refinement is disallowed for dispensationalism, then by the same two criteria covenant theology is discredited. And if these matters are basically nonessential for covenant theology, then they are likewise irrelevant in the critique of dispensationalism.[13]

Of course, the discussion between both dispensationalism and the covenant position has been an engaging one for many decades; but interestingly it appears that the dispensationalists have come closer to the covenantal stance rather than vice versa. This seems to be a logical progression since many of the older dispensationalist, especially those from the decades of the early to mid-twentieth century, were Presbyterian or had connections with universities and seminaries that were Reformed in their theological position. Scofield was within the Congregational denomination while Chafer was ordained within the mainline Presbyterian Church. The basic tenets of Calvinism are accepted, such as the total depravity of humanity, the sovereign determining of God, and the issue of the persevering of the saints. The discussion of the extent of the human will would be open to much debate, as some would hold to a measure of human initiative and ability pertaining to personal choice, while others would hold to the view that the human will is totally incapable of decisions pertaining to ultimate salvation and that only the Spirit could enable such a decision to be efficacious.

Dispensationalism inherently holds to a secret rapture of the saints who are living; this view was prominent in the writings of John Nelson Darby, C. I. Scofield, and Lewis Sperry Chafer, along with many others who held academic positions in colleges, universities, and seminaries, as well as many pastors. However, there has not always been agreement concerning

---

13. Ryrie, *Dispensationalism*, 218.

the time of the rapture or the taking out of the saints. Darby, Scofield, and Chafer, of course, were premillennial and held to the pre-tribulation rapture of the saints—that is, it was believed that they would not go through the time of tribulation, the seventieth week of Dan 9, but they would be taken out before the commencement of this seven-year period.

Another view is typically referred to as the mid-tribulation rapture of the saints—that is, the saints will be caught up before the commencement of the final three-and-a-half years, a time that is believed to be one of unimaginable bloodshed. It is believed that in the middle of the seven-year period, the antichrist will exert complete control and a large number of those who claim Christ will experience martyrdom.

A third understanding of the saints' relationship to this period is the post-tribulation view. The understanding is that the church or the saints will have to go through the entire seven-year period; however, there will be a remnant who will not succumb, and their lives will be spared. At the conclusion of this period, it is believed that the Battle of Armageddon will occur which will be followed by the second advent of Christ who will vanquish the opposition and determine who will enter his millennial reign.

Finally, there is the partial view, which is not held by many. Those who hold to this position claim that only those who are living out the principles of the teachings of the Christian faith and are actively waiting for the second advent will be taken up. This view places a heavy emphasis upon the present sanctification of the regenerate who will be alive at the time.[14]

The Davidic covenant, then, according to the classical view will commence after the completion of the seventieth week of Daniel as recorded in chapter 9 of this Old Testament book. There is no concept that Christ is now reigning on this throne or that he is presently occupying this position. Concerning this matter, Chafer writes, "David was not promised a heavenly, spiritual throne, and the one who contends that David's throne is now a heavenly rule is by so much obliged to name the time and circumstances when and where so great a change has been introduced."[15] Chafer's interpretation had a great influence upon subsequent generations of theologians and pastors in their interpretation of the implications of the Davidic covenant. Chafer gives added insight into the classical dispensational view by writing the following:

---

14. Ryrie, *Dispensationalism*, 172–73.
15. Chafer, *Systematic Theology*, 4:324.

> Since the coming theocratic kingdom is the divine objective with respect to the earth and since it forms the national hope of Israel, the covenant with David which introduces the revelation of the kingdom declares the precise nature of all this. From the inception of the dominate theme onward as seen in subsequent Scriptures the subject is held in constant observation and as a feature of unfulfilled prophecy. The earthly kingdom, the throne, and the King are among the dominate themes of the Old Testament. The revelation respecting these great features in the Davidic covenant is both explicit and extended. Difficulty arises only for those who are determined to metamorphose a literal, earthly throne and kingdom into some vague and wholly imaginary spiritual idealism. The acid test to be applied to any such human notion is the pertinent inquiry of why the King must be of David's line. This evident requirement regarding the King is ignored by every theory which rejects the truth concerning the literal throne and kingdom; yet that the King must be born of David's lineage is both asserted and assumed throughout the great highway of prediction—consider, for example, John 7:42, which states: "Hath not the scripture said, that Christ cometh of the seed of David, and out of the town of Bethlehem, where David was?" God said to David, "And thine house and thy kingdom shall be established for ever" (2 Sam. 7:16).
> ... In this context, which records the words of Jehovah more fully respecting this covenant with David, the literal character of the covenant is assured, the certainty of its fulfillment and the reservation about chastisement are all clearly stated.[16]

Chafer's position still has a large constituency of adherents to this view concerning the Davidic Covenant. The issue in a sense also relates to theodicy. The argument is that Jesus cannot be on the throne now because of the problem of evil and all the ramifications of this in the present human condition and turbulent world affairs. If Jesus were truly reigning, so the argument goes, the gospel would be more readily accepted, evil would not be as rampant, the church would be more united, and Christians would be experiencing a greater measure of victory in their personal lives. Of course, the view is also connected intimately with the understanding of the millennium as a literal, earthly reign of Christ and not simply a spiritual kingdom, as historically promoted by especially covenant theologians.

---

16. Chafer, *Christology*, 321–23.

The new covenant is also an issue that has elicited misunderstanding between the classical and progressive dispensationalists. This covenant is recorded in Jer 31:31–34 and states:

> Behold, the days are coming, declares the LORD, when I will make a new covenant with the house of Israel and the house of Judah, not like the covenant that I made with their fathers on the day when I took them by the hand to bring them out of the land of Egypt, my covenant that they broke, though I was their husband, declares the LORD. For this is the covenant that I will make with the house of Israel after those days, declares the LORD: I will put my law within them, and I will write it on their hearts. And I will be their God, and they shall be my people. And no longer shall each one teach his neighbor and each his brother saying, 'know the LORD,' for they shall all know me, from the least of them to the greatest, declares the LORD. For I will forgive their iniquity, and I will remember their sin no more. (ESV)

Chafer along with most classical dispensationalists understand the covenant as currently unfilled and not to be completed until the one-thousand-year earthly reign of Christ in the future. He adamantly states the following:

> Reference at this point is to the new covenant yet to be made with Israel and not to the new covenant now in force in the Church. All unconditional covenants—the Abrahamic, the Palestinian, the Davidic—since they rest on the faithfulness of God and not at all on the unfaithfulness of men, are unbreakable by men. They endure forever. However, Jehovah made a conditional covenant with Israel when He took them by the hand to lead them out of Egypt (Ex. 19:5; Deut. 29:1). That covenant related to the daily life and conduct of Israel. When Jehovah brings Israel out of the nations and into their kingdom glory, He will make a new covenant with them—not to supersede any unconditional covenant, but to supersede the law covenant which they have broken. . . . If note is taken of the four blessings which this covenant promises, it will be seen that these—and vastly more—are the present possession of those who comprise the Church.[17]

Chafer, then, held that the new covenant is yet to be completely fulfilled; the promise is primarily to Israel and not to the church. This covenant too is held to be unconditional by the majority of classical dispensationalists—that is, the fulfillment will occur despite human failure and sinfulness.

---

17. Chafer, *Systematic Theology*, 4:325.

The progressive dispensational view, however, is that the new covenant has already been fulfilled or at least greatly initiated. There is an "already but not yet" concept in the thinking of some progressive dispensationalists in that the covenant is being fulfilled and will be completed in the future millennium. Progressive dispensationalists, then, hold that both the Davidic and new covenants have been fulfilled; they are either partially yet to be completed or not totally completed but will be done progressively, especially the new covenant.

Ryrie, a classical dispensationalist, of course is critical of the progressive dispensational understanding of the fulfillment of the new covenant. He is convinced that the promises contained within the covenant point to a future completion and only secondarily to the present situation. He states,

> Progressives view the new covenant (like the Davidic covenant) as *already* inaugurated by Christ, who is dispensing certain of its blessings in this age, even though its provisions will *not yet* be fully realized until the Millennium. Furthermore, the new covenant will be mediated by the Davidic King, since the new covenant is a form in which the Abrahamic covenant blessing will be fulfilled. Exactly how this can be established is unclear, though what it intends to establish seems to be an attempt to interrelate the major covenants of Israel under the supremacy of the Davidic King (and the Davidic covenant) as well as making the Abrahamic and the new covenants progressively fulfilled so that the Davidic can be said to be fulfilled also. Even if the Abrahamic and/or the new covenant has been inaugurated, that does not prove that the Davidic has been.[18]

The progression from classical dispensationalism to the progressive position appears to be a predictable movement. As previously cited, many of the early theologians were solidly within the Reformed position, though their eschatological views were viewed as suspect and in some situations even heretical.

The relationship between Israel and the church is a major area of discussion and disagreement especially between dispensationalists and those who hold to a covenant position concerning the two. Classical dispensationalists have historically held to a distinction between Israel and the church.

---

18. Ryrie, *Dispensationalism*, 200.

Chafer, believing in biblical divisions as inherent within the Scriptures, understands that there are four major groupings within the Old and New Testaments. These particular groups consist of the following: angels, gentiles, Jews, and Christians. Chafer is adamant that each one of these entities will retain their identities throughout time. He claims that they will not merge into another group or change their special essence. Rather, each group is distinct, individual, and perpetual.

Many Old and New Testament Scriptures are cited to explicate the nature of the angels. He states that they are created beings whose activity is both on earth and in heaven. Chafer explains that Matt 25:41 substantiates that angels are classified throughout time as angels and they do not change into another kind of being.[19] In his *Systematic Theology* he writes,

> The angels are reported to be present from creation and on into the eternity to come. Under a comprehensive fivefold division of God's finite creatures, as they now exist, the angels comprise two divisions, namely, the holy angels and the fallen angels. To these are added the Gentiles, the Jews, and the Christians. However, all classes of beings, regardless of the order or time of beginning, being originated and constituted as they are, go on in their group distinctions into eternity to come. There is no evidence that other orders of finite beings will be introduced in this age or future ages.[20]

Concerning their dispensational importance, Chafer does not dwell extensively on angels. His primary concern is to enable others to become aware of their existence, perpetuity, and biblical role.

The gentiles are a significant subject for Chafer, and to this group he devotes much attention. He summarizes this group by stating they had their origin in Adam, they have been involved in the fall as recorded in Gen 3, and as subjects of prophecy they will share with Israel, though subordinate to that people, in the coming kingdom. Chafer cites Acts 10, 11, and 13 to give credibility to his belief that gentiles also are a part of the elect group that God is calling out during this present age. But he emphasizes that the mass of gentiles will reject the offer of grace and this group, also known as the nations in the Bible, will be present during the tribulation upon the earth. He believes that the gentiles will be judged at the termination of this period; this group is designated as the goats in Matt 25:31–46, and they are distinguished from the sheep. The latter are heirs of eternal life while the

---

19. Chafer, *Dispensationalism*, 19–20.
20. Chafer, *Systematic Theology*, 4:4.

former is not. Chafer stresses that this is not the last judgment but will only determine who will enter the kingdom, the one-thousand-year reign of Christ upon the earth. The final judgement will be an event which occurs at the termination of the kingdom period, according to Chafer. He succinctly summarizes the period of the gentiles by writing the following:

> Thus it is disclosed that—in spite of the fact that a dispensation of world-rule is committed to them, that in this age the gospel is preached unto them with its offers of heavenly glory, that in the coming age they share the blessings of the kingdom with Israel, and that they appear in the future ages—they remain Gentiles, in contradistinction to the one nation Israel, to the end of the picture; and there is no defensible ground for diverting or misapplying this great body of Scripture bearing on the Gentiles.[21]

According to Chafer, "Though neglected more than any other, the highway of prophecy concerning the Gentiles is one of the most extensive of highways; it is as essential to a right understanding of the prophetic Scriptures as any other, and is earlier in human history with respect to its beginning than the previous one."[22] Chafer believes "Daniel is given the complete review of the history of the Gentiles, beginning with the Jews' captivity and running on into the kingdom age. The period between the captivity and the second advent of Christ is named by him 'the times of the Gentiles.'"[23] Chafer continuously stresses that the prophets, such as Daniel, who wrote of the gentiles did not see the intercalation time of the church or the present time, which has been occurring since the first century AD. He believes that this age simply was not revealed to the Old Testament prophets—in particular, it was not revealed to Daniel.

The third group that Chafer discusses were the Jews. He traces their lineage to Abraham and emphasizes that they have distinct qualities. He believes that although they have been oppressed for many years without their own land, they will one day be a victorious people. "Their rightful king, the Son of David, will occupy the Davidic throne forever (Ps. 89:34–37); Isa. 9:6–7; Jer. 33:17; Luke 1:31–33; Rev. 11:15)."[24]

Chafer believes the Bible teaches that during this present age there is no difference between the Jew and gentile spiritually; they are either

21. Chafer, *Dispensationalism*, 22–23.
22. Chafer, *Systematic Theology*, 4:47.
23. Chafer, *Systematic Theology*, 4:330.
24. Chafer, *Dispensationalism*, 22–23.

with or without grace. "The present divine purpose is the out calling from both Jews and Gentiles of that company who are the Bride of Christ, who are, therefore, everyone to partake of His standing, being in Him, to be like Him, and to reign with Him on this earth (Rev. 20:4, 6; 22:5)."[25] At the completion of this present age, Chafer believes that Israel must pass through the Great Tribulation, and he draws this conclusion from such passages as Jer 30:4-7, Dan 12:1, and Matt 24:21. He claims that this period will begin with the judgments of God upon the earth. The millennium will ensue immediately after the tribulation and according to Chafer is described in Zech 14:1-21. He states that Rev 20:7-15 depicts the ending of the one-thousand-year period. Chafer gives more insight into his thinking concerning the Jewish nation:

> As indicated before, Israel in all her generations—exclusive of those who have entered into the exalted privilege of the present age of grace—will come up for judgment, some to everlasting life and others to everlasting contempt (cf. Dan 12:2; Ezek 20:33-34; Matt 24:37—25:30). The portion of this people who are destined to enter the kingdom become the "all Israel" who will be saved (cf. Isa 63:1) when the Deliverer comes out of Zion according to God's unalterable covenant (Rom 11:26-27, 29). These, like all other creatures of God, are traced into eternity to come; for the kingdom is "an everlasting dominion" (Dan 7:13-14). Great grace from God will be upon those who enter the land (cf. Ezek 2);44; Rom 11:27).[26]

He articulates that there will be Jews excluded from the land, but Chafer admits it is uncertain what their fate will be. "Whatever this estate thus described may be, it abides forever."[27]

Chafer discusses the fourth group, the church or what he terms "Christians." His explanation relates directly to the issue of the church and Israel. The context of the previous three groupings enables one to have a fuller understanding of this topic. Chafer writes, "This company—composed of Jews and Gentiles who are saved and safe in Christ—is never divided in the divine purpose. They are one body.... All sectarian divisions of the Church ... are violence against this unity.... The entire notion that some believers

---

25. Chafer, *Dispensationalism*, 30.
26. Chafer, *Systematic Theology*, 4:416-17.
27. Chafer, *Systematic Theology*, 4:417.

are, through their supposed merit, better than other believers is an insult to that grace which perfectly saves."[28]

The purpose of God is presently centered in this group and the Scriptures addressed to this company include the Gospel of John, the Acts, and the Epistles. The Synoptic Gospels, Chafer believes, present Christ as loyal to the Mosaic law under which he lived. Jew and gentile, then, are one spiritually; there is no difference between them as they are both in Christ. Chafer believes "it is seen, also, that in this new body wherein Jews and Gentiles are united by a common salvation, the middle wall of partition—the agelong enmity between Jew and Gentile—is broken down, itself having been 'slain' by Christ on the cross, thus making peace (Eph 2:14–18)."[29]

Thus, Chafer writes that God distinguishes between groups in the dispensation of law and will again in the kingdom age. But during this present age of grace, the church is comprised of both Jew and gentile.

Classical dispensationalists, such as Chafer, hold to a distinction between Israel and the church. Of course, classical dispensationalists believe that the church is comprised of both believing Jews and gentiles but that Israel, the chosen people of God, is distinct from the church. The understanding is that the beginning of the church is recorded in Acts 2; thus, there is no true church in the Old Testament; Israel is viewed as God's distinct people and the church is viewed as unknown by the Old Testament saints.

Perhaps the central issue of dispute between classical and progressive dispensationalists is the hermeneutical method held by each one. Both believe in the necessity of studying and using the original languages of Hebrew and Greek; thus, exegesis is seen as of paramount importance. Classical dispensationalist historically hold to a historical-grammatical method of interpretation. Of course, they believe that the Scriptures contain figures of speech, and these must be acknowledged and interpreted. However, they are opposed to a method that endorses and uses a spiritual method of interpreting and understanding a particular passage of Scripture, believing that such a procedure leads to a myriad of interpretations and not the original sense of the meaning of a select passage in its context. Ryrie states,

> Dispensationalists claim that their principle of hermeneutics is that of a literal interpretation. This means interpretation that gives every word the same meaning it would have in normal usage, whether employed in writing, speaking, or thinking. It is sometimes called

28. Chafer, *Systematic Theology*, 4:418.
29. Chafer, *Systematic Theology*, 4:12.

the principle of *historical-grammatical* interpretation since the meaning of each word is determined by grammatical and historical considerations. The principle might also be called *normative* interpretation since the literal meaning of words is the normal approach to their understanding in all languages. It might be designated *plain* interpretation so that no one receives the mistaken notion that the literal principle rules out figures of speech. Symbols, figures of speech, and types are all interpreted plainly in this method, and they are in no way contrary to literal interpretation. After all, the very existence of any meaning for a figure of speech depends on the reality of the literal meaning of the terms involved. Figures often make the meaning plainer, but it is the literal, normal, or plain meaning that they convey to the reader.[30]

Most dispensationalists would agree with Ryrie's broad assessment of the hermeneutical and exegetical basis of interpretation. Such an approach seems logical, biblical, consistent, and a means for determining the meaning of the message in its historical context and how the interpretation would apply to the contemporary situation and setting.

However, representatives of the progressive dispensational position argue that this explanation, though meaningful, is woefully lacking in a total understanding of how to interpret the Bible and, in particular, various genres of Scripture. Blaising and Bock argue for a fuller comprehension of Scripture, which is possible through a more thorough method. They acknowledge that the historical-grammatical hermeneutic has been historically adopted by many; however, they raise the question of what this method actually means. They see the procedure as somewhat cursory and incomplete. They state,

> In fact, evangelical scholars have been comfortable for some time describing their approach to interpretation as the historical-grammatical method. It means pursuing initially the meaning of the author/Author as expressed in the text with a sensitivity to its original textual setting. It means that reading for what it means to me may miss what the text meant and means. But what exactly does such a reading involve?[31]

The authors continue an extended discussion concerning what they see as a weakness in classical dispensationalism's hermeneutical approach to the

---

30. Ryrie, *Dispensationalism*, 91 (emphasis original).
31. Blaising and Bock, *Progressive Dispensationalism*, 76–77.

interpretation of Scripture. The attempt for a more thorough approach is reflected in the following summary of their approach:

> We will survey the approach in three categories: (1) the historical, (2) the grammatical, and (3) the literary-theological. These are three components in assembling the portrait of the meaning of Scripture, and we will examine them in three distinct subsections. Again we break up into pieces what is really an interactive, dynamic process. Think of these three sections as separate overlays that together form a picture on an overhead. This reflects the multidimensional aspect of interpretation. First, the historical level seeks to be sensitive to the message as it came to its original audience, understanding original terms and ideas. Second, the grammatical level considers how the terminology of that message is laid out. Terms are not understood in isolation from each other but in conjunction with one another. Third, the literary-theological level highlights the fact that there is an abiding message and unity in the text, which is laid out literarily in various ways called genres. Each genre presents truth in its own way and makes unique demands for how it should be read. Reading the Bible requires an awareness of the changing nature of the terrain within the text, as well as an appreciation of the various angles used to present the truth.[32]

Their approach is representative of the revised method of interpretation for those who hold to a form of dispensational theology. Classical dispensationalists claim that they have a method, and for sure they do, but certainly their hermeneutical structure is quite simplistic in comparison to the revised system of progressive dispensationalism.

Ryrie admits that since the publication of his book on dispensationalism in 1965, the field of hermeneutics has changed; he states that there are approximately three developments in the area of hermeneutics: linguistics, genre-centered study, and one's pre-understanding as one attempts to interpret the Scriptures.[33]

Blaising and Bock believed that the classical method is outmoded and in need of major revisions. They claim,

> Hermeneutics has become much more complex today than when Charles Ryrie affirmed literal interpretation as the "clear, plain, normal" method of interpretation. Perhaps we can explain it this way: Ryrie set up an equation: dispensationalism = literal

---

32. Blaising and Bock, *Progressive Dispensationalism*, 77.
33. Ryrie, *Dispensationalism*, 89–90.

> interpretation = clear-plain-normal hermeneutics = grammatical-historical interpretation. Then he claimed that only dispensationalists practiced consistently literal interpretation. If a person practiced consistently literal interpretation (as defined by the equation) then he or she would be a dispensationalist. Furthermore, a number of dispensationalists who today practice consistent grammatical-historical interpretation (in its more developed sense) have revised some of the distinctive interpretations of earlier dispensationalism. Literary interpretation has developed so that some things which earlier interpreters thought they "clearly" saw in Scripture, are not "clearly" seen today at all. This raises a question both about the meaning of "literal" interpretation and the claim that its consistent practice is the essence of dispensationalism. It seems that "literal" is often used to mean the system and tradition of revised dispensationalism. But traditional dispensationalism must always be tested by ongoing historical-literary interpretation as that interpretation develops in its understanding, methods, and procedures. It must, that is, if one remains committed to Scripture as the primary authority of theology. When we read Ryrie's claim that consistently "clear, plain, normal" hermeneutics is the essence of dispensationalism, we have to interpret the remark historically. It may have been true as an ideal or goal for revised dispensationalism, but the statement is not true as a comprehensive principle inclusive of classical dispensationalism. . . . Consequently, Ryrie's remark, even though it failed as a description of dispensationalism's unchanging essence, nevertheless pointed to a direction in which dispensational hermeneutics was to develop. The old principle of spiritualization has been left behind, and dispensationalists, first revised and then progressive, have pursued the goal of consistent historical-grammatical hermeneutics even as they developed it in meaning and method in consultation with other evangelicals.[34]

Blaising and Bock raise many salient points regarding the need for a more clear and consistent hermeneutic. They even believe that the term "grammatical-historical" does not have the same meaning today as it did in the mid-twentieth century, and that it is thus an anachronism.

---

34. Blaising and Bock, *Progressive Dispensationalism*, 36–37.

Critique of Progressive Dispensationalism

Classical dispensationalism has been extant for about 150 years; however, progressive dispensationalism is indeed a newcomer in reference to theological movements. Many cite the origins of progressive dispensationalism as November 20, 1986, in connection with the Evangelical Theological Society meeting in Atlanta, Georgia. Over the years interested professors and students continued to gather to discuss the proposed revisions for classical dispensationalism. The term "progressive dispensationalism" was suggested at the Evangelical Theological Society meeting in 1991, and discussion revolved around "significant revisions" in dispensational theology.[35] Ryrie writes that the differences in the revised theological position are not minor but are to be considered as major reconstructions. He states,

> In an attempt to justify their movement away from normative dispensationalism, progressives have pointed to differences in some interpretations among normative dispensationalists. They conclude that, if normatives can do it, their revisions are justified also. However, the crucial consideration is not that there are some differences, but what those differences are. Are they minor or major? In general, differences in interpretations and emphases among normative dispensationalists do not change the overall system of dispensationalism, whereas the differences advanced by progressive do form a new and revised system that some (both dispensationalists and nondispensationalists) believe is not dispensationalism anymore.[36]

The debate continues between the revisionists and the traditionalists. This has also been a cause for some criticism especially from those who are thoroughly Reformed in their theological position. Even though dispensational thought contains many of the tenets of Reformed theology, historically there has been at times much heated debate between representatives of both theological stances. Chafer engaged in much discussion within his own denomination, Presbyterian Church USA, concerning dispensationalism. Of course, Presbyterian theology is thoroughly Reformed, and dispensationalism during Chafer's time and even currently is viewed as a theological position that is not amenable with Reformed doctrine.

A discussion of some of the historical issues concerning the criticism of dispensationalism would be helpful at this point. Chafer, though ordained

---

35. Ryrie, *Dispensationalism*, 189–90.
36. Ryrie, *Dispensationalism*, 189–90.

as a Presbyterian, did not believe *The Westminster Confession of Faith* was as clear as Scripture concerning his particular theological position, which of course was dispensational. He gives a summary of his thought concerning the controversy between dispensationalism and covenant theology, writing,

> Because past, present and future ages (cf. Eph 1:10; 3:1–6) are so clearly seen in the Scriptures, covenant theologians acknowledge different ages or time-periods, but then they treat them as merely different ways of administering one and the same divine purpose. Regardless of every feature known to earlier ages, it will be seen that the Word of God builds all its doctrinal structure on an age past, a present age, and a future age. To deny these varied divisions, however, gathered as they are about the different revealed purposes of God, is to cease to be influenced duly by the precise Scripture which God has spoken.[37]

James E. Bear, former professor of literature and interpretation of the New Testament at Union Theological Seminary in Richmond, Virginia, aims many remarks at Chafer's dispensationalism. He primarily sees dispensationalism as a recent occurrence in theological thought, stating that the teachings came to America in the 1850s. He states that the premillennial view dates to the early church and that this view was not dispensational premillennialism. He cites the works of Scofield and Chafer and claims that these two had similar dispensational views.[38]

The controversy between representatives of the Presbyterian Church USA and those who held dispensational views such as Chafer was continuous. Chafer gives insight into the debate:

> Of more moment than its own import would indicate is the action of the Presbyterian Church, U.S., at its recent General Assembly by which action an investigation of so-called *dispensationalism* is being conducted. The inquiry, according to the wording of the overture which promoted the investigation, is "as to whether the type of Bible interpretation known as *Dispensationalism* is in harmony with the Confession of Faith." This move on the part of the Presbyterian Church, U.S., will doubtless be observed by other denominations. Since dispensational distinctions form an integral

---

37. Chafer, *Systematic Theology*, 7:123.

38. Bear, "Covenant of Grace," 285–307. Cf. Allis, "Unity of the Scriptures," 22–35; "Law of God," 272–89; and Bowman, "Dispensationalism," 170–86.

feature of the premillennial interpretation of the Scriptures, all premillennialists are challenged by this investigation.[39]

Chafer does not remain silent on the issue, but he engages in defense of his position. For example, he writes the following statement:

> Since there is so much in the [Westminster] Confession of Faith which is in no way related to this discussion and which is the common belief of all, the issue should yet be narrowed to the difference which obtains between *Dispensationalism* and *covenantism*. The latter is that form of theological speculation which attempts to unify God's entire program from Genesis to Revelation under one supposed Covenant of Grace. That no such covenant is either named or exhibited in the Bible and that the covenants which are set forth in the Bible are so varied and diverse that they preclude a one-covenant idea, evidently does not deter many sincere men from adherence to the one-covenant theory.[40]

Obviously exasperated, he states, "It is time for any theological Rip Van Winkle to awaken to the recognition of that which has developed doctrinally since a company of good men drew up the Confession of Faith."[41]

A major charge that Bear raises is that Scofield and Chafer teach two means of salvation: obedience to the law as one means and salvation by grace through faith in Christ as another. Bear states, "We are led to the conclusion, then, that the Dispensational teaching about 'dispensations' gives two methods of salvation, works and grace."[42] Moreover, Bear writes, "Again, let us say, under this heading we are simply emphasizing the fact that the Dispensationalists do not teach one plan of salvation, and here they seem to diverge radically from the teaching of our Church and from the Church throughout the ages."[43] Somewhat sarcastically, Bear concludes his opinion concerning Chafer's dispensationalism: "But we must note further that Dr. Chafer himself feels that it [covenant theology] is widely divergent from the belief held by those who are not of his group. We agree with him that his view is widely divergent form the view held by the Church throughout the ages."[44] Chafer defends himself, stating, "There is, therefore, but one way to

---

39. Chafer, "Distinctives Challenged," 337 (emphasis original).
40. Chafer, "Distinctives Challenged," 338.
41. Chafer, "Distinctives Challenged," 341.
42. Bear, "Covenant of Grace," 297.
43. Bear, "Covenant of Grace," 297–98.
44. Bear, "Dispensationalism and the Covenant," 304–5.

be saved and that is by the power of God made possible through the sacrifice of Christ."[45] A controversial subject during this discussion concerned how salvation was obtained before the time of Christ. Chafer believes,

> God has assigned different human requirements in various ages as the terms upon which He Himself saves on the ground of the death of Christ, is a truth of Scripture revelation and is recognized as true by those who receive their doctrine from the Sacred Text rather than from manmade creeds. Nevertheless, when the various human requirements of the different ages are investigated it is found that they come alike in the end to the basic reality that faith is exercised in *God*. And that one basic element of trust in God doubtless answers that which in every case God must require.[46]

However, concerning this issue, Chafer was not too clear concerning salvation before the time of Christ. For instance, he does not state what the essential element of faith in Christ entails in dispensations before the dispensation of grace; thus, it is somewhat understandable that this lack of clarity caused confusion and controversy.

Sometimes Chafer makes unguarded statements such as the following: "Whatever may have been the divine method of dealing with individuals before the call of Abraham and the giving of the Law by Moses, it is evident that, with the call of Abraham and the giving of the Law that followed, there are two widely different, standardized, divine provisions, whereby man, who is utterly fallen, might come into the favor of God."[47] Chafer claims that this statement led to much "misunderstanding and unjust criticism."[48] He explains that the word "salvation" is not in the statement he wrote. He claims that he is simply stating the truth that some have come into a relationship with God, as is the case of Israel and Judaism, by a physical birth and others, as is the situation with Christians in Christianity, by a spiritual birth. Concerning the subject of salvation, Chafer writes, "But the determination persists that those who hold to dispensational distinctions teach there are two ways to be saved. What they really teach, if at all, is that Judaism had its requirements summed up in the works of the Law of Moses, which system, or religion, is not now in effect, and that Christianity has its requirements summarized in faith and is now the one and only basis

---

45. Chafer, "Misunderstanding," 1.
46. Chafer, "Misunderstanding," 2 (emphasis original).
47. Chafer, "Dispensationalism," 410.
48. Chafer, "Two Ways to Be Saved?," 1.

of acceptance with God."[49] However, it does appear that Chafer could have been clearer concerning the content of pre-Christ faith and the ultimate ground of salvation after the advent of Christ.

Having touched on some important historical discussions and controversies, there are many views on how to revise classical dispensationalism. One initially gains the impression that the progressive dispensationalists were more cutting-edge and perhaps had accrued more highly recognized graduate degrees; many had studied especially in Scotland and Germany. While this was not necessarily an argument for more validity on the part of the progressive dispensationalists, it could lead to the conclusion that the progressive wing are not sufficiently acquainted with the theological position of those who hold to the historic dispensational, premillennial theological position. However, while many classical dispensationalists have held academic positions for decades, many of their writings did not reflect a deeper appreciation for linguistics and the variety of genres of Scriptures. Blaising and Bock even detail approaches for engaging in a more comprehensive manner of reading the Scriptures, which are as follows: historical-exegetical, biblical-theological, and canonical-systematic. Concerning specifically the canonical-systematic approach, the authors state,

> Another theme that draws on this type of dynamic reading is the development of kingdom texts in the Bible. The journey moves from its formation in promise to Israel and David to its culminating description in terms of millennium and then the new heaven and new earth. The Old Testament mostly discusses the promise of a kingdom on earth (2 Sam 8–16), with the exception of brief remarks in Daniel that suggest a heavenly origin (esp. Dan 2 and 7). The New Testament develops these heavenly elements of the hope (Eph 2:4–7; Phil 3:20; Heb 12:22–24), culminating in the Millennium and then the new heaven and new earth (Rev 20–22). When Revelation is read canonically-systematically, its message refracts back on Old Testament kingdom texts to show that the promised kingdom is fulfilled in part within the Millennium and the new heaven and new earth. What Old Testament promises have not been fulfilled yet will be fulfilled in the future. As the Apostle Peter suggests, there is much detail about the career of Jesus and the outworking of promise declared in the Old Testament (Acts 3:21). To appreciate how the entire story unfolds and which promises belong where, one must read the text *historically-exegetically*, *biblically-theologically*, and *canonically-systematically*. All three

49. Chafer, "Two Ways to Be Saved?," 1.

levels are appropriate, though ultimately the canonical-systematic reading brings the pieces of the Bible's message together.[50]

Obviously, the hermeneutical structure of progressive dispensationalism is more comprehensive. However, classical dispensationalists understood and employed a method that was suitable for the time in which they did their research.

Progressive dispensationalists have significantly modified the standard understanding of dispensationalism. Critics of the revised theological position may have viewed the changes as minor, significant, or even extreme. Those who hold the changes are extreme would state that the revision is no longer truly dispensationalism but is very similar to Reformed theology.

The understanding of the Davidic covenant has been significantly revised, and with the emphasis upon the current reign of Christ, many would believe that the progressive dispensationalists have modified their premillennial view to one of amillennialism, or are at least going in this direction. Ryrie summarizes succinctly the differences between the two theological stances:

> Beginning in the 1980s a group from within the dispensational camp have been promoting significant changes in normative, or traditional, dispensationalism. The tenets include the following: (1) the kingdom of God is the unifying theme of biblical history; (2) Christ has already inaugurated the Davidic covenant and is now reigning in heaven on the throne of David (right hand of the Father = the throne of David); (3) the concept of two purposes and two peoples of God (Israel and the church) is not valid; (4) thus, the church is not a separate group of redeemed people, nor was it unrevealed in the Old Testament (just unrealized); (5) there is one divine plan of holistic redemption for all people and all areas of human life (personal, societal, cultural, and political).[51]

Conclusion

This chapter discusses the origins of progressive dispensationalism. The three who are recognized as the theologians who proposed the revised stances are Craig A. Blaising, Darrell L. Bock, and Robert L. Saucy. All three have written extensively concerning progressive dispensationalism and are widely viewed as the original figures of the revised position. Their academic

50. Blaising and Bock, *Progressive Dispensationalism*, 101–2 (emphasis original).
51. Ryrie, *Dispensationalism*, 79.

credentials, research and teaching experience, especially within the dispensational camp, and other factors are viewed and interpreted as credible and certainly innovative.

It is well documented that historically there are many highly regarded dispensationalists, many of whom were either in a Reformed denomination or had close connections to groups that had a close affinity to such a theological stance. Many, such as Poythress, argue that progressive dispensationalism is so close to Reformed theology that the position should actually be called such! Other are more conciliatory and believe that theological positions even within set doctrinal borders morph and evolve, but the revisions are still to be viewed as intimately related to the originally-held beliefs and constructs.

The four major areas of revisions discussed are the following: the Davidic covenant, the new covenant, the church and Israel, and the hermeneutical foundation. Obviously, there have been significant revisions and interpretations. Overall, it appears that the revisionists are still within the dispensational position, but the issues have been revised to such an extent that to avoid confusion on the part of many, a new term for the revisionists could be helpful to use; a term such as "Reformed millennialism" would be seen perhaps as more concise and conciliatory.

Chapter Three

Interpretations of the Kingdom

Historic Interpretations of Classical Dispensationalism

AUGUSTINE IS USUALLY CITED as the father of amillennialism. He is considered by many to be one of the greatest church fathers; many consider him to be one of the major theologians in the history of the church. He began to acquaint himself with the epistles of Paul and had a dramatic conversion experience. Augustine was baptized by Ambrose on Easter in the year 387 A.D. He entered the priesthood, and for many years he was the bishop of Hippo in North Africa. He was a prolific writer; his two best-known works are *Confessions* and *The City of God*. His influence has been enormous in the fields of theology and philosophy.[1]

Weber writes, concerning Augustine's influence on millennial views,

> Bishop Augustine of Hippo (354–430) marks the turning point in Christian millennial thought, and most Christians since have appreciated his approach to prophetic and apocalyptic texts. A mild millennialist in his early days, Augustine eventually rejected both apocalyptic millennialism and Eusebius's view of church and empire, which was untenable after the sack of Rome by Alaric in 410. Instead of arguing that the Parousia ushers in a new kingdom, Augustine believed that the city of God and the city of man coexist through time but remain completely separate. Earthly kingdoms

---

1. Virkler and Ayayo, *Hermeneutics*, 54–55.

come and go, but the city of God endures forever. In that way, Augustine countered the charge that Christianity had weakened the once-invincible Roman empire and thus caused its fall to more robust barbarians. He also argued that because the Christian's true citizenship is in God's city, the fall of Rome made little difference in the scheme of things. *The City of God* (XX.7–20), then, developed a new way of understanding apocalyptic prophecies. While not discussing the historical reality of the coming Antichrist and the chaos at the end of the age, Augustine made no attempt to find current fulfillments or identify signs of the times. Apocalyptic texts were not just about historical events: they also described the Church's ongoing struggle with good and evil and the spiritual battle that raged in the heart of every Christian. Thus, like Origen before him, Augustine understood Revelation allegorically. The millennium in chapter 20 refers to the time between Christ's first and second comings. He reigns now with his "resurrected" saints, both in heaven and in the city of God. Augustine believed that Christ had already bound the devil for the church, but Satan's power in the earthly city was still strong. Augustine still expected the Second Coming, the final revolt and defeat of Satan, and the last judgment; but his allegorical approach to texts and his assertion that redemptive and secular history were not fundamentally related dealt a severe blow to the older reading of prophetic and apocalyptic texts.[2]

Premillennialism, then, had been the usual manner in understanding the unfolding of history eschatologically. The early church, though premillennial, of course was not dispensational. Augustine believes the thousand years

> can be interpreted in two ways. It may indicate that this event happens in the last thousand years, that is, in the sixth millennium, the sixth day, as it were, of which the latter stretches are now passing, and a Sabbath is to follow that has no evening, the rest, that is to say, of the saints, which has no end. Thus, our author used the term 'a thousand years' to denote the last part of the millennium—or 'day'—which remained before the end of the world, employing the figure of speech by which the whole stands for the part. Alternatively, he may have intended the thousand years to stand for the whole period of this world's history signifying the entirety of time by a perfect number. For, of course, the number 1,000 is the cube of 10, since 10 multiplied by 10 is 100, a square

---

2. Weber, "Millennialism," 370–71.

but plain figure, but to give height to the figure and make it solid 100 is again multiplied by 10, and we get 1000.³

Augustine's view, then, would eventually be the dominant view. Of course, he predated sixteenth-century theologians such as Luther and Calvin, who essentially followed Augustine's views. Weber believes, however, that millennialism was kept alive through a small but influential minority who had such leaders as Isaac Newton in England and Johann Albrecht Bengel in Germany.⁴

In the latter years of the nineteenth and early twentieth centuries there were three theologians associated with Princeton who exerted a powerful influence upon postmillennial thought. The three were Charles Hodge, Archibald A. Hodge, and Benjamin B. Warfield.

Charles Hodge (1797–1878) graduated from Princeton in 1815 and from the seminary in 1819. He became an instructor at Princeton in 1820 and remained there his entire life. He was a professor of biblical literature from 1822–40 and professor of theology for his remaining years. His writings carried his influence far beyond the three-thousand students he taught. His most influential work was his *Systematic Theology* (1872–73), which is still in print and is considered a classic in Reformed theology.

He begins his division of the second advent with a general outline of his eschatology:

> The common church doctrine is, first, that there is to be a personal, visible, and glorious advent of the Son of God. Secondly, that the events which are to precede that advent, are
>
> 1. The universal diffusion of the Gospel; or, as our Lord expressed it, the ingathering
> 2. of the elect; this is the vocation of the Christian church.
> 3. The conversion of the Jews, which is to be national. As their casting away was
> 4. National, although a remnant was saved; so their conversion may be national,
> 5. although some may remain obdurate.
> 6. The coming of Antichrist.
>
> Thirdly, that the events which are to attend the second advent are:

---

3. Augustine, *City of God*, 907–8.
4. Weber, "Millennialism," 375.

DAVIDIC MILLENNIALISM

1. The resurrection of the dead, or the just and the unjust.
2. The general judgment.
3. The end of the world. And
4. The consummation of Christ's kingdom.[5]

Hodge does not mention the binding of Satan (Rev 20:1–31). The closest he comes to mentioning God's opposition to Satan is the coming of antichrist. He believes that there are different uses of the word "antichrist," but in the book of Revelation he understands it to refer to the ecclesiastical power of the papacy.

Hodge believes that the Bible speaks of only one general resurrection. He cites three categories of passages as proof: (1) passages where the righteous and the wicked are raised together (John 5:28–29, Matt 25:31–32, Rev 20:12–13, and 2 Thess 1:7–10); (2) passages which teach that the resurrection of the righteous will take place at "the last day" when Christ shall appear in glory; therefore, there is not a thousand years before that event (John 11:24; 6:39–40, 44, 54; 12:48); and (3) passages which teach that the resurrection of the saints will take place at the day of judgment or the final judgment (Matt 24:30–31, 25:31–46; 2 Tim 1:7–10).[6] Hodge believes Christ will come a second time, the dead in Christ will rise, all nations will be judged, and the present order of things will cease.[7] Hodge claims the possible exception to only one general resurrection is Rev 20:4–6. He also admits that the passage taken by itself seems to teach two resurrections. But he gives six reasons why he thought this passage should not be interpreted as two literal resurrections. This interpretation, of course, goes against the dispensational premillennial understanding of the passage.

He believes that the kingdom will be brought in gradually. He states the following:

> It is not only asserted that the kingdom of Christ is to attain this universal extension by slow degrees, but its gradual progress is illustrated in various ways. Our Lord compares his kingdom to a grain of mustard-seed, which is indeed the least of all seeds, but when it is grown it is the greatest among herbs; and to leaven which a woman took, and hid in three measures of meal, till the whole was leavened.[8]

5. Hodge, *Systematic Theology*, 792.
6. Hodge, *Systematic Theology*, 840–41.
7. Hodge, *Systematic Theology*, 840.
8. Hodge, *Systematic Theology*, 856.

INTERPRETATIONS OF THE KINGDOM

God has always had a kingdom on earth, according to Hodge, and the messianic form began when the Son of God became flesh. Hodge further believes that "nothing, therefore, can be more opposed to the plain teaching of the New Testament, than that the kingdom of Christ is yet future and is not inaugurated until his second coming. This is to confound its consummation with its commencement."[9] Hodge believes that the number one thousand is symbolic; therefore, according to him, it does not necessarily point to a literal period.

> This period is called the millennium because in Revelation it is said to last a thousand years, an expression which is perhaps generally understood literally. Some however think it means a protracted season of indefinite duration, as when it is said that one day is with the Lord as a thousand years. Others, assuming that in the prophetic language a day stands for a year, assume that the so-called millennium is to last three hundred and sixty-five thousand years. During this period, be it longer or shorter, the Church is to enjoy a season of peace, purity, and blessedness such as it has never yet experienced.[10]

Hodge describes this glorious estate of the church prior to the second coming:

> As therefore the Scriptures teach that the kingdom of Christ is to extend over all the earth; that all nations are to serve Him; and that all people shall call Him blessed; it is to be inferred that these predictions refer to a state of things which is to exist before the second coming of Christ. This state is described as one of spiritual prosperity; God will pour out his Spirit upon all flesh; knowledge shall everywhere abound; wars shall cease to the ends of the earth, and there shall be nothing to hurt or destroy or destroy in all my holy mountain, saith the Lord. This does not imply that there is to be neither sin nor sorrow in the world during this long period, or that all men are to be true Christians. The tares grow together with the wheat until the harvest. The means of grace will still be needed; conversion and sanctification will be then what they ever have been. It is only a higher measure of the good which the Church has experienced in the past that we are taught to anticipate in the

---

9. Hodge, *Systematic Theology*, 857.
10. Hodge, *Systematic Theology*, 858–59.

future. This however is not the end. After this and after the great apostasy which is to follow, comes the consummation.[11]

Hodge is not without his detractors. George N. H. Peters believes that Hodge borrowed heavily from two persons' works: Dr. Brown's *Christ's Second Coming* and Barnes's *Revelation*.[12]

Archibald Hodge, son of Charles Hodge, graduated from Princeton in 1846, and after a short period as a missionary in India, he returned to America and entered the pastorate. He was a professor of theology at Western Theological Seminary in Allegheny, Pennsylvania, and served there until 1877. From 1878 until his death in 1886, he served as professor of theology at Princeton Seminary.

A. A. Hodge's eschatology is seemingly identical to his father's views. He claims that the following events must occur before the second advent: antiChristian apostasy, the preaching of the gospel to every nation, the fullness of the gentiles, the conversion of the Jews, the millennial prosperity of the church, and the final defection.[13] He believes that the millennium will be a thousand years, in which period the gospel will have great influence over the entire earth.[14] But the influence of the gospel will be gradual:

> The Scriptures, both of the Old and New Testament, clearly reveal that the gospel is to exercise an influence over all branches of the human family, immeasurably more extensive and more thoroughly transforming than any it has ever realized in time past. This end is to be gradually attained through the spiritual presence of Christ in the ordinary dispensation of Providence, and ministrations of his Church.[15]

The younger Hodge believes that all the dead, good and bad, are to rise and be judged at the second advent.[16] Concerning the kingdom, he writes,

> As to the fact that the kingdom of Christ has already come. He has sat upon the throne of his Father David ever since his ascension. . . . The Old Testament prophecies, therefore, which predict this

---

11. Hodge, *Systematic Theology*, 859.
12. Peters, *Theocratic Kingdom*, 3:244.
13. Hodge, *Outlines of Theology*, 568.
14. Hodge, *Outlines of Theology*, 568–69.
15. Hodge, *Outlines of Theology*, 568.
16. Hodge, *Outlines of Theology*, 571.

INTERPRETATIONS OF THE KINGDOM

kingdom, must refer to the present dispensation of grace, and not to a future reign of Christ on earth in person among men in the flesh.[17]

Charles Hodge and his son Archibald Hodge are essentially identical in their eschatological views. Both exert an enormous influence especially in Reformed denominations.

Benjamin B. Warfield (1851–1921) graduated from Princeton Seminary in 1878 and was appointed professor of New Testament literature and exegesis at Western Theological Seminary in Allegheny, Pennsylvania. In 1887 he became a professor of theology at Princeton Theological Seminary, where he succeeded A. A. Hodge. He served in this capacity for thirty-three years.

Warfield records principles he believes were important for understanding the book of Revelation and prophecy in general:

1. *Recapitulation and successive visions*—Warfield claims that it is exegetically untenable to view the book of Revelation as one continuous progressive vision. He believes that it is a series of seven, with each reaching to the end, not in mere repetition of one another but unfolding an ever-increasing development.

2. *Symbolism*—He claims that the language of the Apocalypse has its own laws of interpretation.

3. *Ethical purpose*—It is the spiritual and ethical impression that rules the presentation and not an annalistic or chronological intent.

4. *Fulfillment of prophecy*—The fulfillment of prophecy is to be separated. It is only when one understands the book fully can one answer with certainty the question of fulfillment.[18]

Warfield believes that it is necessary to picture the nineteenth and twentieth chapters of Revelation as a complete unit. He writes,

> The picture of this conquering church is given us in the nineteenth chapter. But there is also the church waiting there above, but not waiting merely, but living and reigning with Christ, free from all strife and safe from all assaults of the evil one. This is depicted for us in the opening verses of the twentieth chapter. Not the one only, but both together—the church militant and the church

---

17. Hodge, *Outlines of Theology*, 570.
18. Warfield, "Millennium and Apocalypse," 601.

expectant—constitute the church of Christ; and not the one alone but both together pass unscathed through the great trial (latter part of ch. XX) to inherit the new heavens and new earth (ch. xxi).[19]

Warfield pictures chapter 19 of Revelation as the church engaging in battle and gaining victory by the means of preaching the gospel. He states,

> We are not to think, as we read, of any literal war or manual fighting, therefore, the conquest is wrought by the spoken word—in short, by the preaching of the gospel. In fine, we have before us here a picture of the victorious career in the Gospel of Christ in the world. All the imagery of the dread battle and its hideous details are but to give us the impression of the completeness of victory. Christ's gospel is to conquer the earth: He is to overcome all His enemies.[20]

From the quote, clearly Warfield believes in a "golden age" for the church. In one of his articles, he mentions various views of premillennialism and postmillennialism. In this article, Warfield strongly suggests that he was a postmillennialist.[21]

How did Warfield understand the thousand years of Rev 20:3?

> The thousand years, thus, is the whole of this present dispensation, which again is placed before us in its entirety, but looked at now relatively not to what is passing on earth but to what is enjoyed "in paradise." This, in fact, is the meaning of the symbol of a thousand years. For, this period between the advents is, on earth, a broken time—three and a half years, "a little time" (ver. 3)—which, amid turmoil and trouble the saints are encouraged to look upon as a short duration, soon to be over. To the saints in bliss it is, on the contrary, a long and blessed period passing slowly and peacefully by, while they reign with Christ and enjoy the blessedness of holy communion with Him—"a thousand years."[22]

He understands that the number one thousand symbolizes in the Bible a time period of absolute perfection and completeness. Warfield explains,

> The sacred number seven in combination with the equally sacred number three forms the number of holy perfection, ten, and when this ten is cubed into a thousand the seer has said all he could

19. Warfield, "Gospel and Second Coming," 349.
20. Warfield, "Millennium and Apocalypse," 602.
21. Warfield, "Gospel and Second Coming," 349–51.
22. Warfield, "Millennium and Apocalypse," 604–5.

say to convey to our minds the idea of absolute completeness. It is of more importance, doubtless, however, to illustrate the use of five-periods to convey the idea of completeness. Ezek. xxxix. 9 provides the instance.[23]

Warfield, then, believes the "thousand years" symbolizes heavenly completeness and blessedness, and the "little time" symbolizes earthly turmoil and evil.

Warfield's understanding of the "binding of Satan" is as follows:

It is a description in the form of a narrative: the element of time and chronological succession belongs to the symbol, and not to the thing symbolized. The "binding of Satan" is therefore, in reality, not for a season, but with reference to a sphere; and his "loosing" again is not after a period but in another sphere; it is not sequence but exteriority that is suggested. There is, indeed, no literal "binding of Satan" to be thought of at all: what happens, happens not to Satan but to the saints, and is only represented as happening to Satan for the purposes of symbolic picture. What actually happens is that the saints described are removed from the sphere of Satan's assaults.[24]

Warfield also understands the first resurrection as spiritual. The martyrs of Rev 20:4 are symbols for all of Christ's saints in the world. It is those saints who have died and now are in paradise with the Lord that Warfield calls the first resurrection.[25] The second resurrection Warfield interprets as literal. He writes, "The 'first resurrection' is here, therefore, the symbolic description of what has befallen those who while dead yet live to the Lord; and it is set in contrast with the 'second resurrection,' which must mean the restoration of bodily life."[26]

Warfield admits the difficulty with his interpretation of Rev 20:1–10 lies with the word "nations." The word normally represents the anti-Christians in the Apocalypse. However, Warfield thinks that the word "nations" may have a double sense like the word "world." Therefore, he understands "the 'nations' here, not of the anti-Christian world in contrast with the

---

23. Warfield, "Millennium and Apocalypse," 608–9.
24. Warfield, "Millennium and Apocalypse," 605–6.
25. Warfield, "Millennium and Apocalypse," 607.
26. Warfield, "Millennium and Apocalypse," 607.

Christian, but of the world on earth in contrast with the saints gathered in paradise."[27]

Warfield seemingly has both amillennial and postmillennial views: "We are forced, indeed, to add our assent to Kleiforth's conclusion, 'that the doctrine of the thousand-year kingdom has no foundation in the prophecies of the New Testament, and is therefore not a dogma but merely a hypothesis lacking all Biblical ground.' The millennium of the Apocalypse is the blessedness of the saints who have gone away from the body to be at home with the Lord."[28]

But conversely, it is challenging to place him in the amillennial camp since, after he denied the earthly millennium, he claims that his view of the millennium does not deny a "golden age" in a spiritual sense for the church in the future. The vision of the latter half of chapter 19 of the book of Revelation emphasizes that the gospel is to completely subdue the world. The gospel will be preached to the whole world before the second advent, but the winning of the world will not most likely eliminate all evil.[29]

He summarizes this point: "There is a 'golden age' before the Church—at least an age relatively golden gradually ripening to higher and higher glories as the Church more and more fully conquers the world and all the evil of the world; and ultimately an age absolutely golden when the perfected Church is filled with the glory of the Lord in the new earth and under the new heavens."[30]

Charles Hodge, Archibald A. Hodge, and Benjamin B. Warfield exercise a great influence upon Reformed theology. Many segments of their views are both accepted and rejected by especially classical dispensationalists, many of whom had been intimately familiar with the theological training and backgrounds of especially these three highly regarded theologians. Remarkably, progressive dispensationalism is much more accepting of the theological conclusions of these three; of course, classical dispensationalists would still be skeptical especially of the hermeneutical method of interpretation, specifically of the use of a spiritual and not a literal understanding of various prophecies, events, and resurrections, and the spiritual interpretation of key words.

---

27. Warfield, "Millennium and Apocalypse," 611.
28. Kleiforth, quoted in Warfield, "Millennium and Apocalypse," 615.
29. Warfield, "Millennium and Apocalypse," 616.
30. Warfield, "Millennium and Apocalypse," 616.

INTERPRETATIONS OF THE KINGDOM

Select Passages

There are select passages in the New Testament that have been interpreted differently by scholars. Classical dispensationalists have interpreted the Sermon on the Mount as pertaining primarily to the one-thousand-year earthly reign of Christ during a literal kingdom on earth. This interpretation has obviously caused much discussion since their understanding of the passage is that it is not for the church today but is for those who have entered this kingdom—that is, it is strictly for a future time and has nothing to do with the present age. The various interpretations have even stated the passages in the Sermon on the Mount teach that salvation is by the means of works and not faith. Harnack writes that Jesus appears to state in the Sermon on the Mount "the several departments of human relationships and human failings so as to bring the disposition and intention to light in each case, to judge man's works by them, and on them to hang heaven and hell."[31]

Interestingly, progressive dispensationalists abandon the classical dispensational view. Blaising and Bock write,

> Much of Jesus' teaching was given in the form of parables. Since the kingdom of God was the major topic of His preaching, it is not surprising that many of the parables concern this subject and its related themes. We cannot undertake a major study of parables in these pages. Rather, we want to note Jesus' teachings on *mysteries of the kingdom* which appear to give new revelation about the kingdom beyond that which we have seen so far. Included in the new revelation was the prediction of a form or stage of the kingdom's presence prior to its full and apocalyptic establishment. This new stage does not appear to be the presence of the kingdom in Jesus' own Person as was discussed earlier (although the epistles will link these concepts together). *While it is not altogether clear in the parables that this newly revealed presence of the kingdom will follow the cross, it is clear that it is a stage which precedes the apocalyptic coming of the kingdom.*[32]

Blaising and Bock discuss several of the parables such as the parable of the wheat and tares (Matt 13:24–30), the parable of the sower (Matt 13:3–9), the parable of the mustard seed (Matt 13:31–32), and the parable of the leaven and meal (Matt 13:33). The authors argue that wheat and tares are in this current time; the former represent those who are regenerate while

---

31. Harnack, *What Is Christianity?*, 72.
32. Blaising and Bock, *Progressive Dispensationalism*, 251 (emphasis original).

the latter are representative of those who are not. Explaining the parable of the wheat and the tares, Jesus says that the "sons of the kingdom" will be coexisting with the "sons of the evil one." Blaising and Bock state that this particular parable appears to state a present application: "

> The coming of the Son of Man at the conclusion of this passage is consistent with Jesus' teaching elsewhere about the Son of Man coming in an apocalyptic manner, executing judgment and instituting the kingdom of God. What is different, however, is the phrase "they will gather *out of His kingdom* all stumbling blocks." This would appear to identify a situation *before* the coming of the Son of Man as *His kingdom*. Both those who belong to Him and those who will be condemned are present in that form of kingdom. After His coming, only the saved will be present in the kingdom. Both conditions, before and after His coming are called "kingdom." Since the kingdom phase prior to this coming is the only new teaching in this parable, it would appear to be the "mystery of the kingdom of heaven" which the parable gives us. It is not a kingdom from that which follows, but a phase, a *mystery form* of the same kingdom.[33]

Thus, clearly progressive dispensationalism renounces the classical views, especially those of Scofield and Chafer who are adamant that the parables have allusions strictly to a future time and could be understood by means of application to the present situation. Chafer especially firmly states that to believe in the present fulfillment of the kingdom was a great error in theological discussion and beliefs. Chafer succinctly summarizes this point by stating, "One of the greatest errors of theologians is an attempt, as essayed now, to build a kingdom on the first advent of Christ as its basis, whereas according to the Scriptures it will be realized only in connection with the second advent. All Scriptures conform to this arrangement, strange though it may look."[34] Ladd summarizes Chafer's view with the following summary:

> The kingdom because it was rejected and postponed, entered a mystery form (Matt 13) for this present age. This mystery form of the kingdom has to do with the church age when the kingdom of heaven is embodied in Christendom. God is now ruling on earth in so far as the parables of the mystery of the kingdom of heaven require. In this mystery phase of the kingdom good and evil mingle together and are to grow together until Christ returns. . . .

33. Blaising and Bock, *Progressive Dispensationalism*, 252–53 (emphasis original).
34. Chafer, *Systematic Theology*, 7:224.

INTERPRETATIONS OF THE KINGDOM

The millennial kingdom will then be realized as Christ returns in power and glory at the conclusion of the tribulation. Then Israel, which has been gathered from its dispersion throughout the earth to her covenanted land, Palestine, will recognize the returning Christ as her Messiah, will accept him as such, and will enter the millennial kingdom as the covenanted people.[35]

The distinctions, then, between classical and progressive dispensationalists are clear concerning the kingdom. There is a certain present reality of the kingdom according to the newer movement; they believe that the Scriptures are clear in supporting their position. The older of the two, classical dispensationalists, are convinced that though there is a foretaste of the kingdom now, Christ is not ruling; thus, he is not seated on the throne of David as predicted in 2 Sam 7.

At this point, it is helpful to define more clearly the kingdom of God. Classical dispensationalists traditionally distinguish between the kingdom of heaven and the kingdom of God, claiming that the former alludes to God's rule over the earth in the future earthly millennium, while the latter is in reference to his sovereign reign over time and history. Ladd, however, offers this definition: "The kingdom of God is the sovereign rule of God, manifested in the person and work of Christ, creating a people over whom he reigns, and issuing in a realm or realms in which the power of his reign is realized."[36] Ladd gives further insight by stating, "Yet while God is the King under whose sovereign control the world of nature and men exist, there is a sense in which God's reign is not actualized in human history. By virtue of the fall, mankind has turned aside from the will of God and experience of his gracious reign."[37] Progressive dispensationalists, then, appear to be more in line with Ladd's views than with classical dispensationalists. Ladd presents a balanced view since he was critical of both the amillennial and dispensational views.

The interpretation of the Davidic covenant is a litmus test for how one views the current ministry of Jesus. Classical dispensationalists believe that the fulfillment of the promise as contained in 2 Sam 7:12–17 will not be fulfilled until a future time. Chafer believes that "difficulty arises only for those who are determined to metamorphose a literal, earthly throne and

---

35. Ladd, *Crucial Questions*, 51.
36. Ladd, *Crucial Questions*, 80.
37. Ladd, *Crucial Questions*, 81.

kingdom into some vague and wholly imaginary spiritual idealism."[38] The solely futuristic view of the kingdom according to Chafer does not mean that God is not involved in human affairs: "Since as earlier defined, the kingdom of heaven is the rule of God in the earth, it follows that it is not present to the extent to which He is exercising authority over the affairs of the *cosmos*."[39] Chafer continues, "The King will be Emmanuel and by human birth a rightful heir to David's throne, Himself born of a virgin in Bethlehem of Judea. Emmanuel's kingdom will be heavenly in character in that the God of heaven will rule in the earth, His will to be done on earth as it is done in heaven.... Emmanuel's kingdom will be realized only by virtue of the power and presence of the returning King."[40]

However, progressive dispensationalists present a different understanding of the fulfillment of the kingdom. Yet Ryrie claims that the progressive representatives are presenting a view that has been extant for a long time:

> This already/not yet bifurcation is not new in theological parlance. Nor is it always used in the two-pronged concept of the Davidic rule (now in heaven, later on earth). Introduced by C. H. Dodd in 1926, it is meant generally that the kingdom of God was already present, even though in some way it was also future. In George Ladd the "already" relates to Christ's reign in salvation and the "not yet" to His future reign in the Millennium. In Hoekema (an amillennialist) it means Christ's present heavenly reign on earth and His future reign in the new heavens and new earth. In Sproul (an amillennialist) the "already" is the present age and the "not yet" is the eternal state. In progressive dispensationalism, the "already" is Christ's present reign in partial fulfillment of the Davidic covenant and the "not yet" is His millennial reign.[41]

Blaising and Bock, representatives of the progressive division of dispensationalism, go into a very detailed discussion of the Davidic covenant, primarily arguing that classical dispensationalists have overlooked many significant aspects of the covenant made with David. The authors write,

> We have traced in some detail the fact that the New Testament presents Jesus' present position and activity as a fulfillment of the

---

38. Chafer, *Christology*, 321.
39. Chafer, *Christology*, 349 (emphasis original).
40. Chafer, *Christology*, 357.
41. Ryrie, *Dispensationalism*, 197.

promises of the Davidic covenant. This has been necessary because earlier forms of dispensationalism tended to deny it. They were concerned to underscore the future fulfillment of the political and earthly aspects of the Davidic promise as that promise interfaces with the political and earthly promises of the other covenants. We need to note that the New Testament does indicate that the political aspects of Jesus' Davidic kingship will be fulfilled in the future. But earlier dispensationalists tended to miss the fact that in biblical theology, *the Davidic nature of Christ's present activity guarantees the fulfillment of all of the Davidic promises in the future, including the national and political dimensions of that promise.*[42]

However, Ryrie continues to counter this conclusion, the view of the present reigning of Christ, by stating,

> Regarding Acts 2–3, progressives argue that, since Peter states that Jesus was exalted to the right hand of the Father and since Jesus is the ultimate heir to the Davidic throne, He must now be reigning as the Davidic king in fulfillment of the Davidic covenant (the right hand of the Father being the throne of David in heaven). . . . Actually what Peter is arguing for is the identification of Jesus of Nazareth as the Davidic king. That will happen in the future millennial kingdom. If it is so *clear* that our Lord is reigning now as the Davidic king in inaugural fulfillment of the Davidic covenant, why is that only *alluded to* [Ryrie is arguing here against word choices used by Blaising and Bock] in Acts 2? Links and similarities between reigns do not make an equality between the Davidic reign and Christ's present rule. . . . If Christ inaugurated His Davidic reign at His ascension, does it not seem incongruous that His first act as reigning Davidic king was the sending of the Holy Spirit (Acts 2:33), something not included in the promises of the Davidic covenant? Furthermore, the writer of Hebrews plainly declares that Christ "sat down at the right hand of the throne of God," not the throne of David (12:2). That does not deny that our Lord has all authority in heaven and earth or that He rules in the world and in the church; rather, it denies that He is ruling on David's throne now and that the Davidic covenant has already been inaugurated. To conclude otherwise confuses various rules in the Bible. Remember, too, that David himself was designated and anointed to be king some time before he began to reign as king. Christ is the Davidic king, designated before His birth to reign

---

42. Blaising and Bock, *Progressive Dispensationalism*, 179–80 (emphasis original).

over "the house of Jacob," not the church (Luke 1:31–33), though He will not be reigning as Davidic king until the second coming.[43]

Both sides presented arguments concerning the present reign of Christ. The classical stance is heavily indebted to John Nelson Darby, C. I. Scofield and Lewis Sperry Chafer whose positions were almost identical. Chafer's massive *Systematic Theology* completed in the late 1940s had a significant influence upon subsequent generations of theologians including C. C. Ryrie. The newer version of dispensationalism interestingly seems to be close to the position of George E. Ladd and Reformed theology in general.

The Church and the Kingdom of God

A litmus test for whether one is dispensational or not concerns the doctrine of ecclesiology or the church. Classical dispensationalism continues to hold to a distinction between Israel and church, claiming that the church is not in the Old Testament and is distinct from Israel. Chafer writes,

> Christ is the Bridegroom and the Church is the Bride. Israel was the repudiated (yet to be restored) wife of Jehovah; the Church is the espoused virgin bride of Christ. This relationship for Christians, foreseen in various types, is all of another sphere and future. It sets for the glory of Christ in which the Church as His Bride will share above. . . . Pauline Ecclesiology is divided into three major divisions of doctrine: (1) the Church which is Christ's Body, His Bride, His fulness (John 1:16; Col 2:9–10), and He is made full in them (Eph 1:22–23); (2) the local church, which is an assembly composed of those who in any locality profess to be followers of Christ; and (3) the high calling for a daily life in conformity with the position which the believer sustains, being in Christ. Along with this is the doctrine of the empowering, indwelling Spirit by whom along the high calling can be realized. It is evident from the Bible that God had a rule of life for Israel which was the Law of Moses, and that He will yet have a legal requirement for them in the future kingdom. . . . It is never taught in the Scriptures that Israel as a nation will appear in heaven, though this destiny is open at present to individual believers from among the Jews. The destiny of the nation is earthly, extending on forever into the new

---

43. Ryrie, *Dispensationalism*, 198–99. Cf. Ladd, *Theology of the New Testament*; Robertson, *Christ of the Covenants*; Hoekema, *Bible and the Future*; Hodges, "Acts 2"; Toussaint, "Contingency of the Kingdom."

INTERPRETATIONS OF THE KINGDOM

> earth which is yet to be. The destiny of the Church is heavenly. As His Bride and Body, the Church will be with the Bridegroom and Head wherever He goes.[44]

Chafer gives the following details because he believes the church was future to the ministry of Christ: "There could be no Church until it was purchased with His precious blood (Eph 5:25–27), until He arose to give it resurrection life (Col 3:1–3), until He ascended to be the Head over all things to the Church (Eph 1:20–23), or until the Spirit came on Pentecost through whom the Church might be coordinated by His indwelling presence."[45]

The issue of the church has been a major point of contention with those who hold to an amillennial view of the kingdom. For example, Charles Hodge argues that the church was founded on the covenant made with Abraham.[46] Clarence Bass claims, "Whatever evaluation history may make of this movement [classical dispensationalism], it will attest that dispensationalism is rooted in Darby's concept of the church—a concept that sharply distinguishes the church from Israel."[47] Classical dispensationalists, of course, argue that the church did not begin until the coming of the Holy Spirit as cited in Acts 2; thus, the distinction between Israel and the church is a significant point of controversy between the amillennial and classical dispensational views.

However, Ryrie argues that this is not the case with the progressive dispensational stance. Ryrie believes,

> The nature of the church is a crucial point of difference between classic, or normative dispensationalism, and other doctrinal systems. Indeed, ecclesiology, or the doctrine of the church, is the touchstone of dispensationalism (and also pretribulationism). Not only has the dispensational teaching concerning the church been the subject of controversy, but also the ramifications of that teaching in ecclesiastical life have been attacked. Antidispensationalists, rather than examining the validity of dispensational teaching on this subject, simply dismiss it as heretical.[48]

Blaising and Bock are critical of the manner in which classical dispensationalists view and describe the church as an intercalation, a parenthesis,

---

44. Chafer, *Systematic Theology*, 7:129–30.
45. Chafer, *Systematic Theology*, 7:128.
46. Hodge, *Systematic Theology*, 549.
47. Bass, *Backgrounds to Dispensationalism*, 127.
48. Ryrie, *Dispensationalism*, 143.

in God's program; they argue that in a sense this view makes the church almost an afterthought and not a vital aspect of God's program for the ages. They explain the differences by stating the following:

> Like earlier dispensationalists, progressive dispensationalists view the church as a *new manifestation of grace*, a new dispensation in the history of redemption. Earlier dispensationalists viewed the church as a completely different kind of redemption from that which had been revealed before or would be revealed in the future. The church then had its own future separate from the redemption promised to Jews and Gentiles in the past and future dispensations. Progressive dispensationalists, however, while seeing the church as a new manifestation of grace, believe that this grace is precisely *in keeping with* the promises of the Old Testament, particularly the promises of the new covenant in Isaiah, Jeremiah, and Ezekiel. The fact that these blessings have been inaugurated in the church distinguishes the church from Jews and Gentiles in the past dispensation. But only *some* of those blessings have been inaugurated. Consequently, the church should be distinguished from the next dispensation in which *all* of the blessings will not just be inaugurated, but completely fulfilled (which fulfillment will be granted to the saints of all dispensations through the resurrection of the dead). One of the striking differences between progressive and earlier dispensationalists, is *that progressives do not view the church as an anthropological category in the same class as terms like Israel, Gentile Nations, Jews, and Gentile people. The church is neither a separate race of humanity (in contrast to Jews and Gentiles) nor a completing nation (alongside Israel and Gentile nations), nor is it a group of angelic-like humans destined for the heavens in contrast to the rest of redeemed humanity on earth. The church is precisely redeemed humanity itself (both Jews and Gentiles as it exists in this dispensation prior to the coming of Christ.*[49]

The doctrine of ecclesiology historically has not been given as much attention in many segments of Protestantism as have the other major doctrines, such as theology proper, christology, pneumatology, bibliology, soteriology, and eschatology. Reformed theologians believe that it is more wholistic and concise to see the church throughout the Old Testament and with the call of Abraham initiating the special relationship that God has with His people. This has caused many to see the dispensational understanding as disjointed and incongruous. Indeed, Augustine was a primary

---

49. Blaising and Bock, *Progressive Dispensationalism*, 49 (emphasis original).

influence in arguing against the early church's understanding of the millennium as connected with an ecclesiastic system. Ladd believes "Augustine's doctrine of the City of God banished the millennial interpretation of the Kingdom from the realm of dogmatic Catholic theology."[50]

Rather than discuss Reformation ecclesiology, Erickson gives an insightful conclusion concerning the membership of the invisible church, writing,

> We have argued that while the form the people took in the Old Testament was national Israel, in the New Testament it is the church, and that church began with Pentecost. Does this mean that we who are now part of the church will be forever in a separate grouping from the Old Testament believers? I would suggest, instead, that those were part of Israel prior to Pentecost have been incorporated into the church. This certainly seems to have been the case with the apostles. They had been part of Israel, but at Pentecost became the nucleus of the church. If the Old Testament believers, those who made up true Israel, were saved, like the rest of us, on the basis of Christ's redemptive life and death, then they may well have been swept by the event of Pentecost into the same body as the New Testament believers. Israel was not, then, simply succeeded by the church; Israel was included within the church. The people of God are truly one people; the body of Christ is truly one body.[51]

Coming from a Reformed tradition, Grudem believes,

> both Protestant and Catholic theologians outside of the dispensational position have said that the church includes both Old Testament believers and New Testament believers in one church or one body of Christ. Even on the nondispensational view, a person may hold that there will be a large-scale conversion of the Jewish people (Rom. 11:12; 15:23–24, 25–26, 28–31), yet that this conversion will result in Jewish believers becoming part of the one true church of God—"they will be grafted back into their own olive tree" (Rom. 11:24). . . . Moreover, the present church age, which has brought about the salvation of millions of Christians in the church, is not an interruption or parenthesis in God's plan, but a continuation of his plan expressed throughout the Old Testament to call a people to himself. Paul says, "For he is not a real Jew who is

---

50. Ladd, *Crucial Questions*, 24; cf. MacCulloch, *Reformation*, 184. MacCulloch argues that B. B. Warfield gave great insight into Reformation theology by stating that "the sixteenth-century Reformation was a struggle within the mind of Augustine."

51. Erickson, *Christian Theology*, 1058.

one outwardly, nor is circumcision something external and physical. *He is a real Jew who is one inwardly*, and real circumcision is a matter of the heart, spiritual and not literal" (Rom. 2:28–29). Paul recognizes that though there is a literal or natural sense in which people who are physically descended from Abraham are to be called Jews, there is also a deeper or spiritual sense in which a "true Jew" is one who is inwardly a believer and whose heart has been cleansed by God.[52]

Dispensationalists, whether classical or progressive, do not identify the church with the kingdom. The church is "*in* the world but not *of* the world." This truth is represented by the imagery of being the wheat among the tares, waiting for the final day of redemption. Classical dispensationalists understand that there is a separate program for the church and Israel—the church's destiny is heaven while Israel's is a renewed earth.

Ryrie argues that progressive dispensationalism is more in agreement with the amillennial understanding of the church. For example, Oswald T. Allis, a Humboldt University, Berlin, graduate, believes that the "mystery" of the church "was new and unknown in a relative sense only, being in its essentials an important theme from the time of Abraham."[53] Ryrie states that a similar view is also found in covenant premillennialism as represented by J. Barton Payne, and even in progressive dispensationalism as contained in the writings of Robert L. Saucy.[54] Both Payne and Saucy argue that even though the church is not fully revealed in the Old Testament, there is enough revelation for the Old Testament saints to realize that they were in a special covenantal relationship with God. Of course, classical dispensationalists claim that the doctrine of the church was totally unknown to those in such a relationship with God, and the church was revealed only in the New Testament era, specifically as detailed in Acts 2.

Ryrie believes that the progressive dispensationalists had presented a very different understanding of the church from the classical view. He states there are at least four areas in which the shift has occurred in their new approach: (1) the understanding of the church as merely redeemed humanity; (2) in redefining the view of mystery of the church; (3) in denouncing the view of the church as an intercalation or a parenthesis in

---

52. Grudem, *Systematic Theology*, 861 (emphasis original).

53. Allis, *Prophecy and the Church*, 97.

54. Ryrie, *Dispensationalism*, 154; cf. Payne, *Imminent Appearing*, 126; Saucy, "Mystery of God," 144.

God's program; and (4) a different view of the meaning of the baptism with the Holy Spirit.[55] The baptism with the Holy Spirit particularly is a diverging point from classical dispensationalism, which has understood pneumatology or the subject of the Holy Spirit as different in both the Old and New Testaments. They hold that in the Old Testament, the Spirit came upon certain persons for a specific need or circumstance, but that filling was only temporary, whereas in the New Testament it is believed that the Spirit enters into the one who has experienced a new birth in Christ. Saucy articulates the change with the progressive dispensational perspective by writing the following:

> The recognition that Spirit baptism belongs to all of the participants of the new covenant, including the nation of Israel when it turns to the Messiah, raises the question how to apply the images or metaphors associated with the present work of God in the church. This question is especially important in relation to the metaphor of the body. According to the apostle Paul, baptism with the Spirit forms the body of Christ (1 Cor 12:13). The body, in turn, is frequently identified with the church (e.g., Eph 1:22–23; Col 1:18). From this we could conclude all participants in the new covenant, including the nation of Israel, are included in the church as the body of Christ and therefore any distinction between Israel and the church—which is at the heart of the dispensationalism interpretation—is prohibited. And what can be said of the body would seem to apply to the other images of the church also.[56]

Ryrie especially has an issue with Saucy's view, stating, "Progressive dispensationalists do not believe the baptism is a unique ministry only for the people of the present church age and understand the body metaphor as applicable to believers who are not in the church."[57]

Clearly, then, there is a great variance in ecclesiology between the classical and progressive dispensational view. Some may argue that theological interpretations are not static, there is continuous interpretations and reinterpretations even of the basic doctrines and Scriptures. Classical dispensationalists may have seen the new interpretation as a concession to the present culture and other methods of hermeneutics with which they are not comfortable. Still others may view the discussion as one between generations and that classical dispensationalists were using methods and

---

55. Ryrie, *Dispensationalism*, 153–57.
56. Saucy, *Progressive Dispensationalism*, 183–84.
57. Ryrie, *Dispensationalism*, 157.

patterns simply handed down by many who neither knew nor appreciated other hermeneutical procedures.

Conclusion

Augustine in his *City of God* initiates the position that the kingdom is not future but is a present reality; this stance heavily impacted the medieval church and the Reformers, and continues to the present in much of Protestantism, especially in Reformed denominations, theological schools, and churches. There are several Princeton professors who continued the amillennial interpretation such as Charles Hodge, A. A. Hodge, and B. B. Warfield. Charles Hodge believes in a literal second advent of Christ. His *Systematic Theology* is still in print and is one of the standard texts in many divinity schools, especially those of the Reformed position. He seemingly has some postmillennial views as well since he held that the diffusion of the gospel would be universal before the second advent. Hodge has varying views of the antichrist, as he claimed that there are different uses of the word. He holds to one resurrection, though he does admit that Rev 20:4–6 was an exception in that the passage could be interpreted to teach two resurrections. Believing that the kingdom will come in gradually and not through a cataclysmic event, he seemingly holds to a mixture of both amillennial and postmillennial views.

A. A. Hodge's positions are almost identical with those of his father. Though the influence of the kingdom will be gradual, he claims the kingdom is already in progress. He especially believes the Old Testament is a source for a present and future understanding of the unfolding of history.

Benjamin B. Warfield does much work on the book of Revelation, concluding that it is possible to understand the book as one continuous revelation. Claiming the series of seven is one key to interpretation, he holds to a more symbolic interpretation of the book. Like A. A. Hodge, he too has some postmillennial nuances in his understanding of eschatology.

Historically, classical dispensationalism has been somewhat critical of the three Princeton theologians' understanding of the kingdom. However, progressive dispensationalists appears to be much more appreciative of their views.

Classical dispensationalists believe that the Sermon on the Mount and its relevance is not for the church today. Rather, the interpretation is that this biblical passage describes the spiritual atmosphere of the kingdom era.

However, progressive dispensationalists have abandoned this view of the Sermon on the Mount; they view the message as applicable for today. The same is true also of the various parables that the classical branch of dispensationalism has historically believed are not directly applicable to the present age; the progressive wing does not accept this. They understand the parables are pertinent for contemporary times.

The progressives believe that the kingdom is active now. Christ is reigning, and the church is not merely experiencing a foretaste of the kingdom promises. This division of dispensationalism also does not distinguish between the kingdom of God and the kingdom of heaven as earlier dispensationalists did.[58]

The Davidic covenant is one of the key factors distinguishing these two branches of dispensationalism. The older division continues to hold that the covenant is not fulfilled; the new wing has moved to a more Reformed stance, believing that Jesus is now seated on the throne of David and is actively engaged in fulfilling the promise as contained in 2 Sam 7. This is a significant difference, in that the view that he is now reigning impacts the concept of the millennium. It could be argued that this is a pre-John Nelson Darby perspective and a return to what many would claim is the historic understanding of the church. Some would argue that there are obvious inconsistencies with such a view. For example, what is seen as rampant evil in the present world seems in the thinking of many to mitigate against the belief that Jesus is fully reigning. The area of theodicy, or the question of why evil persists, as well could be discussed as therein is, according to some, a glaring contradiction concerning the sovereign reign of Christ in the present.

The older branch of dispensationalism continues to hold to the separation of Israel and church, each with its own program, culminating in an earthly and heavenly completion respectively. Charles Hodge argues that the church has its origins with the covenant made with Abraham, whereas classical dispensationalists believed that the church was founded according to the coming of the Holy Spirit as contained in Acts 2. Blaising and Bock hold to the understanding that the older view of dispensationalism makes the church almost an afterthought with its insistence that the church is an intercalation or parenthesis in God's prophetic time table. The new wing of dispensationalism, as represented by Robert Saucy, argues that even though the church was not fully developed or understood by the Old Testament

---

58. Blaising and Bock, *Progressive Dispensationalism*, 19.

saints, there is enough revelation contained therein for a semblance of the doctrine to be understood. This new understanding is seemingly a concession to Reformed theology. Many of the earlier dispensationalists came from a theological background steeped in Calvinism; thus, it is somewhat ironic that the new generation of theologians who are not as extensively indoctrinated in Reformed theology have, if not reverted to a full acceptance of the view, displayed concessions to Reformed theology in the area of ecclesiology.

Ryrie, who holds to classical dispensationalism, is most critical of the new branch of dispensationalism. Saucy argues that the metaphor of the body of Christ is not only a New Testament one but is contained in the Old Testament as well. Saucy was for many years a classical dispensationalist, but he transitioned to the new movement in his later years.

The new interpretations of both pneumatology and ecclesiology within dispensationalism are at variance with the older view. Those who hold to one or the other view are usually adamantly convinced of their positions.

Chapter Four

Toward a Reconciliation of Views

Strengths and Weaknesses of Classical Dispensationalism

DISPENSATIONALISM SINCE THE TIME of John Nelson Darby has become a very well-known theological position, especially within evangelical Protestantism. C. I. Scofield's *The Scofield Reference Bible* disseminated the position, especially on a popular level. His notes were copious and detailed and influenced especially lay persons to study Scripture in a more serious manner. Some scholars are somewhat critical of his work, such as Ernest Sandeen who argues that Scofield was trained as a lawyer and not a theologian.[1] Sidney Ahlstrom's critique is somewhat more positive concerning Scofield's scholarship.[2] Scofield revised his notes in 1917, and fifty years later, in 1967, after ten years of readjustments, a committee of nine scholars produced *The New Scofield Reference Bible*. Central to Scofield's eschatology is his adamant belief in the distinction between law and grace:

> It is, however, of the most vital moment to observe that Scripture never, in *any* dispensation, *mingles* these two principles. Law always has a place and work distinct and wholly diverse from that of grace. Law is God prohibiting and requiring. Grace is God beseeching and bestowing. Law is a ministry of condemnation; grace, of forgiveness. Law curses, grace redeems from that curse.

1. Sandeen, *Roots of Fundamentalism*, 224.
2. Ahlstrom, *Religious History*, 2:279–80.

> Law kills, grace makes alive.... Everywhere the Scriptures present law and grace in sharply contrasted spheres. The mingling of them in much of the current teaching of the day spoils both; for law is robbed of its terror, and grace of its freeness.[3]

Scofield does not believe that the present age of grace, the church age, was known to the Old Testament prophets. The Gospels, then, he holds, have no relationship to the church. Scofield believes,

> The Gospels do not unfold the doctrine of the Church. The word occurs in Matthew only. After His rejection as King and Saviour of the Jews, our Lord, announcing a mystery until that moment "hid in God" (Eph 3:3–10), said "I will build my church" (Mt. 16:16–18). It was, therefore, the future; but His personal ministry had gathered out the believers who were, on the day of Pentecost, by the baptism with the Spirit, made the first members of "the church which is his body" (1 Cor 12:12–13; Eph 1:23).[4]

Scofield continues this line of reasoning, stating, "Christ is never called King of the Church. 'The King' is indeed one of the titles, and the Church in her worship joins Israel in exalting 'the King, eternal, immortal, invisible' (Ps 10:16; 1 Tim 1:17). But the Church is to reign with Him. The Holy Spirit is now calling out, not the subjects, but the co-heirs and co-rulers of the kingdom."[5] He also believes that the Scriptures teach that "the Spirit forms the church ... by baptizing all believers into the body of Christ[,] ... impart[ing] gifts for service to every member of the body[,] ... guid[ing] the members in their service[,] ... and is Himself the power of that service."[6]

Scofield insists that the true church is a pilgrim in a world that is not consonant with the purposes of God: "Is the church to take up the work of the rejected king, and to install in the earth the kingdom? What in a word, is the relation of the church to the world? Briefly this: to pass through it a pilgrim body of witnesses."[7]

Lewis Sperry Chafer's views on the kingdom are identical to those of C. I. Scofield. While Scofield is a significant influence on a popular level concerning dispensational theology, Chafer was more academically oriented. His training at Oberlin College was in music, and he did not take

---

3. Scofield, *Rightly Dividing*, 34–35 (emphasis original).
4. Scofield, *Scofield Reference Bible*, 990.
5. Scofield, *Scofield Reference Bible*, 990.
6. Scofield, *Scofield Reference Bible*, 1150.
7. Scofield, *Addresses on Prophecy*, 13.

any courses in theology; however, from an early age, his primary mentor was his father, Thomas Chafer, who was a graduate of Auburn Theological Seminary and a Congregational pastor. Lewis Sperry Chafer was the author of several books that were well received and widely read. Some of these books, published by the Zondervan Publishing House, include the following: *He That Is Spiritual*; *The Kingdom in History and Prophecy*; *Salvation*; *Satan*; *Grace*; *True Evangelism*; *and Major Bible Themes*. These works along with his lengthy and detailed *Systematic Theology*, as well as his decades of teaching courses in theology, impacted a large segment of those who were his students as well as those who had read his numerous works.

The academic study and dissemination of dispensational theology is also extended through the ministries of many who are professors in various colleges, universities, and seminaries, including the following: Moody Bible Institute, Talbot Theological Seminary, Dallas Theological Seminary, and many lesser-known schools.

Classical dispensationalists are recipients of a method of interpretation that stems back to the mid-nineteenth century. The study of hermeneutics has become much more progressive and sophisticated since this time and has especially become more so in recent decades. Those who hold to the older view of dispensationalism argue this progression and sophistication has enabled especially lay persons to have a method of outlining and understanding basic themes in Scripture, such as the covenants in the Old Testament, prophetic passages, messianic types, and future predictions throughout both the Old and New Testaments. Further, many would state that these methods have enabled a clearer understanding of the mandates of missions, evangelism, and sanctification, encouraging Christians to fulfill these both individually and collectively, especially under the direction of ecclesiastical direction.

Dispensational distinctives have been taught in a variety of ecclesiastical authorities—that is, the teaching has been accepted in a variety of theological environs. Many nondenominational venues certainly have disseminated the classical perspective, but the teaching can be seen also in several Protestant denominations especially in the United States. Many of the older dispensationalists were Presbyterians and therefore Reformed in their theological views; thus, even within classical dispensationalism, there is a semblance of a Calvinistic theological foundation concerning such issues as the human will, sin, salvation by grace through faith, the authority of the Scriptures, and the second advent.

Many have argued that the classical view, with its heavy emphasis upon a literal, grammatical, and historical method of interpretation, lends itself more fully to applying the truths of Scripture to one's personal life; thus, the argument is that such a method of interpretation results in a more fully developed life of sanctification or at least the desire for such. A common saying among those who hold to the older view is, "The Scriptures were not written to us, but they were written for us." The inference of such a statement is that the interpretation and application of select segments of Scripture is meant to be taken in a personal manner and not merely as an exegetical exercise to understand the original intent of the author. Inherent within classical dispensationalism, then, is a pietistic emphasis believing that the truths encountered will impact not only the intellectual understanding but also the heart of the person. It is not uncommon among adherents to hear such phrases as, "the deeper life" of the Christian life.

There are obvious weaknesses of classical dispensationalism. The newer branch, which began in the early 1990s, is an attempt for a revisionism on the part of those who had received their training within the classical stance. Many of the earlier theologians, although persons of considerable ability, character, and influence, did not have formal academic training or were not graduates of highly recognized universities and seminaries. John Nelson Darby attended Trinity College, Dublin, in Ireland; however, he did not take any courses in theology; his course of study was in law. He left the Church of England and joined the Plymouth Brethren. Charles Haddon Spurgeon, pastor of the Metropolitan Tabernacle in London believes that Darby was teaching heresy.[8] C. I. Scofield was also a lawyer, and he was essentially a self-taught theologian. Lewis Sperry Chafer was a graduate of Oberlin College, but his area of study was in music. His father was a pastor, and it is highly probable that he was instructed intensively by him. While the lack of theological education does not necessarily diminish the influence, character, and ability of Darby, Scofield, and Chafer, it is a point of contention for especially the progressive dispensationalists, many of whom are graduates of leading universities in the United States and Europe. However, the most intense criticism comes from those within the Reformed segment of Protestantism. Harold O. J. Brown, cites classical dispensationalism as one of the heresies in the church.[9]

---

8. Grant, *Plymouth Brethren*, 60.
9. Brown, *Heresies*, 65.

Chafer died in 1952, and since that period the science of hermeneutics has changed dramatically. While many evangelicals do not appropriate an existential method of interpretation, especially as seen in the works of Heidegger, Barth, and Bultmann, they have read and are reading works written by them in the decades after the death of Chafer. They have become more aware of diversity in interpretation through the methods of deconstructionism. The older school of dispensationalism continues to hold to a literal, historical, and grammatical method of interpretation while the progressive branch, though not adopting many newer methods, are more tolerant and willing to listen to the opinions of other methods of hermeneutics. For example, Blaising and Bock write, "Literary interpretation has developed so that some things which earlier interpreters thought they 'clearly' saw in Scripture, are not 'clearly' seen today at all. This raises a question about both the meaning of 'literal' interpretation and the claim that its consistent practice is the essence of dispensationalism."[10] Virkler believes that "in the twentieth century, the field of hermeneutics underwent a tremendous paradigm shift.... The new paradigm shift integrates linguistic, philosophical, and sociological perspectives into the interpretive enterprise."[11]

Classical dispensationalism places a distinction between Israel and the church. The argument is that God has an earthly plan for Israel and a heavenly one for the church. Progressive dispensationalists argue that emphasizing the church as a parenthesis in God's program makes the promises of the Davidic covenant of no consequence; there is no immediate application of the covenant to the present age.[12] Many argue that the classical understanding of the flow of divine history appears illogical and even disjointed.

Many believe that classical dispensationalism has been a method of interpretation that has helped innumerable people to seriously study the Scriptures, especially when using Hebrew and Greek. The perception and caricature of the method has historically been heavily criticized by especially those of a Reformed theological position. The belief in a rapture of the saints before the actual second advent of Christ has been referred to as heretical at worst and misleading at best by detractors of the theological method used to come to this doctrinal conclusion. The prominent emphasis on the belief in a future antichrist and the numerous popular books and movies on the topic have also elicited criticism.

10. Blaising and Bock, *Progressive Dispensationalism*, 36.
11. Virkler and Ayayo, *Hermeneutics*, 62.
12. Saucy, *Progressive Dispensationalism*, 26–27.

Strengths and Weaknesses of Progressive Dispensationalism

Though progressive dispensationalism has been a movement with a roughly thirty-year history and has been taken seriously by many, there are still many detractors, both from outside of the theological position and from Reformed groups, though it appears that the latter has been much more agreeable currently than in the past.

The initial revisionist movement of dispensationalism comes from two theological professors who had been indoctrinated firsthand with the theological premises of the classical stance. After they had studied in British universities for doctoral studies, they commenced on revising and expanding the work of not only Scofield and Chafer, but especially Ryrie. Ryrie also holds a doctorate from University of Edinburgh in Scotland, and he had for many decades been one of the major recognized scholars of the older school of dispensationalism. His book *Dispensationalism Today*, written in 1965, was updated and retitled *Dispensationalism*. His best known and best selling work is *The Ryrie Study Bible*. Ryrie is convinced that the newer movement went too far in its reassessment of classical dispensationalism. In Ryrie's summary opinion of the new movement he is doubtful about its potential impact: "Where it [progressive dispensationalism] all will lead and whether or not it will be understood and received by those who have embraced normative dispensationalism, no one knows."[13] Ironically, Ryrie is the theological mentor of both founders of the progressive movement, as they studied with him for their initial theological degree.

The progressive dispensational position has certainly proposed a more advanced and concise hermeneutical methodology. For example, Bock, a progressive, writes the following to illustrate the difference between the classical and progressive methods:

> Here is where our differences lie. It is not in a radically different hermeneutical method, one being literal and the other, not. Rather, *we discuss how best to fit the various pieces of the scriptural puzzle together*. Progressives assert that there is a unified meaning and a unified plan to be found in the Scripture that places continuity and discontinuity at various specific points. Nonprogressives insist on discontinuity as an abiding-defining-comprehensive principle in discussing the plan.

---

13. Ryrie, *Dispensationalism*, 209.

> I have used the example of the Davidic throne throughout this essay to give one detailed example of how the approaches differ. This detail has been the topic of much discussion, and rightly so, since it so nicely shows the different ways progressives and nonprogressives handle the reading of the text. What progressives argue is that the forgiveness of sins and the distribution of the Spirit are part of Jesus' current messianic activity that show his ruling-blessing authority as the promised One of God. More, much more on which dispensationalists agree is yet to come in that rule, when He returns and rules the nations from Jerusalem as God finishes completing the execution of His promise to Abraham, Israel, and the world.
>
> What I am arguing is that this theme appears naturally in New Testament contexts where the Law, Psalms, and/or Prophets are being invoked. It is also found in contexts that are marked by the presence of these themes, Scripture, and/or fulfillment. A more normal (literal) reading of such texts is to connect them to the events being alluded to in the New Testament context, rather than to insist that the Old Testament so limits the definition of the term that only an analogy to the future is present.
>
> I am claiming that a nonprogressive hermeneutic operates at a principal-traditional level and shortchanges the canonical meaning, not because such a reading does not provide for a possible sense of the text or because it affirms a discontinuity I reject, but because the sense for which it argues is not the most normal way to read the New Testament context in which the Old Testament promise appears. A consistently normal and complementary reading of the New Testament context introduces a fresh note of continuity in the progress of revelation without resulting in an alteration of the ultimate meaning of the Old Testament passages. Thus, a progressive dispensational hermeneutic is committed to stable meaning as it is progressively revealed across the canon and across the dispensations, eras which in turn build on one another as an advancing sequence in the promise of God. This is the reason why the view is called progressive dispensationalism.[14]

Rather than emphasizing types and future fulfillments of what are perceived as direct correlations between the Old and New Testaments, the progressives understand that the progression of revelation is central to understanding the eternal plan of God. The progressives have the advantage

---

14. Bock, "Hermeneutics," 97–98.

of a fuller understanding in the area of hermeneutics in comparison to the standard classical method of employing the interpretation of various texts.

The classical dispensational position grew out of the Plymouth Brethren movement, and the initial person who proposed the method of interpretation was John Nelson Darby. The Brethren movement was small and somewhat isolated from other ecclesiastical bodies. While C. I. Scofield was ordained within the Congregational denomination, he was the pastor of small churches. Lewis Sperry Chafer initially was ordained in the Congregational ecclesiastical body, but he transferred his membership to the Presbyterian Church, USA. However, because of his dispensational position, he was often seriously questioned by authorities in this denomination; nonetheless, he maintained his full ordination. While Darby was British, both Scofield and Chafer were American and ministered solely in the United States.

Many of the progressive representatives, on the other hand, were more educated and traveled widely. For example, Darrell L. Bock was a Humboldt Scholar multiple years at Tübingen University. The influence of the progressive wing has a more international appeal and influence than that of the classical position.

Classical dispensationalism has been criticized as somewhat simplistic and even nonacademic by detractors. Some of the criticism appears to be valid. However, the theological position has grown in sophistication as scholars have grappled with the premises, issues, and hermeneutical foundations of classical dispensationalism.

It is to be expected that those who represent the older branch of dispensationalism would be critical of the newer position. Though dispensationalism has a theological relationship to Presbyterianism and to Reformed theology, primarily through the influence of Lewis Sperry Chafer, classical dispensationalism has historically held to the distinction between Israel and the church, arguing that there is a separate program for each. The newer position is such a divergence from the older that it could be argued that progressive dispensationalism is no longer dispensationalism, and that the name progressive dispensationalism is in a sense a misnomer; therefore, some believe that the word dispensationalism should not be used. After all, progressives are arguing that the church is the current reality of the eschatological kingdom, a view which predates the progressive view by about seventy years, as it was contained in the writings of George E. Ladd, a proponent of historic premillennialism. Ryrie argues correctly that progressives identify the church with the kingdom.[15] The question could be raised, should not progressive dispensationalists, then, have another name that would more accurately describe their theology? Of course, those who hold to the progressive view may object to such a statement, arguing that the rudiments of dispensationalism are still inherent within the newer position.

One criticism that has been leveled against the newer view is that classical dispensationalism is a view that is more conducive to the spiritual life or to the issue of sanctification. With its heavy emphasis upon the literal interpretation of select passages of Scripture, it is believed by many that the Scriptures become more personal and conducive to matters not only of the mind but also of the heart. Indeed, Ladd, a critic of dispensationalism, writes the following concerning adherents of the older position: "It is doubtful if there has been any circle of men who have done more by their influence in preaching, teaching and writing to promote a love for Bible study, a hunger for the deeper Christian life, a passion for evangelism and zeal for missions in the history of Christianity. They were men who walked with God. From their influence has come a host of Bible Institutes and Bible conferences."[16] The theme of sanctification is also found in the newer movement, but it is more academically oriented. The source of the progressive position is largely from professors of theology who held academic positions in theological seminaries, whereas the older position, though promoted in such institutions, was primarily seen in the ministries of pastors of a variety of local churches within several denominations and associations. The fine points of interpretation and sophistication are usually not raised in such a context, though of course, there are many who hold academic positions who promote classical dispensationalism. Also, the new version is much discussed in theological guilds and societies such as the Evangelical Theological Society; this was not the situation with the older position of dispensationalism.

Call for a Future Interpretation

There are strengths and weaknesses in both classical and progressive dispensationalism. At first glance, it may appear to some to be a generational issue—that is, the younger scholars perhaps seeing the older view of dispensationalism as obsolete, and those who hold to the older perspective

15. Ryrie, *Dispensationalism*, 195.
16. Ladd, *Crucial Questions*, 49.

viewing the newer one as taking undue liberties with the interpretation of key theological doctrines and biblical texts. In attempting to understand better the differences, one sees it is true that the primary persons promoting dispensationalism were pastors initially; this is the situation with especially Darby and Scofield. Chafer was the son of a minister and himself was a pastor for a period. He later became a professor of theology and president of a theological seminary.

The pastoral emphasis is more obvious in the older version. The progressive position was initiated by academicians, and this is especially the situation with Blaising, Bock, and Saucy. All three hold positions in theological seminaries; thus, hermeneutics and what are deemed to be correct interpretations of the text are of primary importance to them. To many who are of the classical dispensational persuasion, the revised version seems too imbedded in academia and theological scrutinizing. Of course, this is not an argument necessarily against the validity of their views, but only an observation of the genesis and context of the newer position of dispensationalism.

Certainly, it is important to inquire about the goal of history: To what extent do both the Old and New Testaments signify this goal? To Chafer and those who hold to the classical view, the kingdom is understood as entirely future. A representative text explaining this is as follows:

> The Bible teaches that God will ultimately triumph over all sin and rebellion in the earth. This is stated in many passages notably 1 Cor 15:24–28: "Then cometh the end, when he shall have delivered up the kingdom to God, even the Father; when he shall have put down all rule and authority and power. For he must reign, till he hath put all enemies under his feet. The last enemy that shall be destroyed is death. For he hath put all things under his feet. But when he saith all things are put under him, it is manifest that he is excepted, which did put all things under him. And when all things shall be subdued unto him, then shall the Son also himself be subject unto him that put all things under him, that God may be all in all." Thus does the divine record predict the restoration of the universe to its primal blessedness under the unchallenged authority of God, when the Son shall have put down all authority and banished every foe. This purpose, as recorded in the Bible appears in various stages or aspects, all leading with the certainty of the Infinite to the glorious consummation.[17]

---

17. Chafer, *Kingdom in History and Prophecy*, 18.

Chafer believes that the one-thousand-year reign of Christ on earth will be a foretaste of the eternal estate itself. The earth will be restored, and what he believed was the judgment of the nations will assure that only those who belong to the Lord will enter the eternal estate.

The Davidic covenant is a key component in the interpretation of the reign of Christ. As previously noted, dispensationalism has hereditary connections with Reformed theology, as Chafer was ordained within the Presbyterian Church. Reformed theology places a heavy emphasis upon the sovereignty of God—he controls and directs all according to his will, even the human will is believed to be subject to him ultimately in all matters. To insist that Christ is not reigning presently, then, seemed almost a contradiction to the historic theological moorings of dispensationalism. Christ's resurrection and ascension assures that he is with the Father reigning with him; thus, he dictates the flow of history according to the ultimate will of the Father.

The issues of theodicy and the obvious outworking of evil in the present world has been interpreted historically to mean that the kingdom is surely in the future and has no relevance to the presence. However, the questions of why there is continued evil and confusion in the present world has always been discussed with no final solution to the issue other than to conclude that ultimately comprehending the questions related to evil's presence rests in the inscrutable will of God and His plan for the cosmos and each life.

Scofield places a heavy emphasis upon seven dispensations: innocence (from the creation to the fall); conscience (from the fall to the flood); government (from the flood to the call of Abraham); promise (from the call of Abraham to the giving and receiving of the law); law (from the giving and receiving of the law until the death of Christ); grace (from the death of Christ until the second advent); and the future kingdom. Chafer, however, though he holds to the seven, only places an emphasis upon three: law, grace, and kingdom. Progressive dispensationalism has reconfigured the dispensations to the following: past dispensations, present dispensation, and future dispensation. Progressive dispensationalists believe that the purpose for both the church and Israel will be fulfilled in heaven eternally.[18]

There has been, then, a great variance of opinion in the number of dispensations and their naming. With the historic and current controversies concerning dispensationalism, it would be beneficial to rename the

---

18. Blaising and Bock, *Progressive Dispensationalism*, 33–34.

theological position. Since the Davidic covenant is such a prominent factor in the interpretation, another nomenclature or title that would more accurately describe the view is Davidic millennialism. The word Davidic emphasizes the covenant as contained in 2 Sam 7; this is understood as an unconditional covenant made with David and ultimately fulfilled in Christ. Millennialism is also a term which describes the position. This perhaps is more helpful than continuing to use the term "dispensationalism," which has been depicted in many unfavorable ways even by those who hold to very similar positions. In a sense the term evokes a negative emotional response on the part of some. However, the progressive movement is still dispensationalism, though greatly modified.

Since God is sovereign, and since Scripture attests that the atoning death of Christ has taken place and the resurrection of Christ is believed to be a historical fact, as well as his ascension, and since he is presently reigning in heaven, it can be concluded that his reign is now taking place with the full manifestation of his sovereign control to be fulfilled in the future.

An overlooked passage in the debate is the passage in which the apostle Paul writes of the giving over of the kingdom to the Father. The passage states, "The comes the end, when he delivers the kingdom to God the Father after destroying every rule and every authority and power. For he must reign until he has put all his enemies under his feet" (1 Cor 15:24–25 ESV). The Son will display the ultimate authority of the Father. Both classical and progressive dispensationalism with their heavy emphasis upon the Davidic covenant lost sight of what is ultimate—that is, that the kingdom will be granted to the Father.

A new nomenclature, then, would be helpful for dispensationalism. The term "Davidic millennialism" emphasizes the culmination of the kingdom. This term emphasizes the Old Testament Davidic covenant and its fulfillment in Christ presently and in the future.

Conclusion

There are both strengths and weaknesses inherent within classical dispensationalism. For a considerable number of years, the theological position was adopted by many theologians, pastors, and even lay persons. The position led to intense interest on the part of many in a clearer understanding of the flow of biblical history and indeed in eschatology. Prophetic and Bible conferences in the nineteenth and twentieth centuries among lay persons centered around dispensational themes. The theological position was promulgated among various theological seminaries and innumerable books and pamphlets promoted the theological position.

This theological persuasion remained remarkably consistent for over two hundred years. Of course, there were differences in interpretation, especially of future events. Dispensationalism holds to a belief in the taking out of the saints before the second coming, an event which was usually termed the rapture of the church, or the taking up of those saints who are still alive at the time of this event. Of course, this is at variance with the majority view of the church, which continues to hold to only the second coming and not a rapture, or taking away, of the saints before the event of Christ's return. For example, Chafer states, "The Apostle goes on to declare a mystery, or a sacred secret hitherto unrevealed (1 Cor. 15:51–57), namely, that 'we shall not all sleep,' but with essential changes which are wrought in a moment, the child of God goes on in this body to meet the Lord in the air (cf. John 14:1–3; 1 Cor. 15:51–52; 1 Thess. 4:13–18; 2 Thess. 2:1; Hebrews 9:28)."[19]

However, there are disputes concerning the time of the rapture for those who hold to this position. Many believe in a pre-tribulation understanding of the time—that is, that the taking up of the saints will be before the commencement of the seven-year period of tribulation; others understand that the event will be in the midst of the seven-year period, which is termed the mid-tribulation view; still others believe that the saints will go through the time of trial and will not be taken up until the full seven years has run to completion; this view is usually referred to as the post-tribulation position. Thus, though there is a measure of consistency within the classical view, there are still matters of debate on events, dates, Israel and the church, and hermeneutical matters.

Theological thought and procedures are never static; they are in constant flux. Issues of culture and hermeneutics interface constantly. Classical dispensationalism needed revision. Some, such as Ryrie, believe that the revised version is no longer dispensationalism, whereas others understand that new thinking and updates that are consistent with scriptural interpretation were greatly needed.

Of course, a large segment of Protestant theologians view dispensationalism in a negative manner, arguing that the theological position is new in comparison to older views such as the amillennial position, which predated dispensationalism by about 1,400 years! Still others argue that

---

19. Chafer, *Systematic Theology*, 4:395.

historic premillennialism, the view of the early church, which of course predates the amillennial position, is the correct interpretation of the millennium. This view, though premillennial, does not hold that there will be a secret rapture of the saints before the second coming but does hold that the return of Christ will occur before his actual millennial reign.

Classical dispensationalism was the prominent perspective until the revised version was initiated in the early 1990s, and the Scofield-Chafer interpretation was held to be the prominent interpretation with its heavy emphasis upon time periods, dispensations, and how God interacted with humanity during those specific periods. Scofield stresses seven dispensations but, while Chafer believes that was the correct number, he only emphasizes the importance of three of them: law, grace, and kingdom. Dissatisfied with many of the tenets of the classical position, younger scholars who had been instructed in the position studied key passages of Scripture and concluded that there are many issues with the position, which is unclear at best and false at worst. Their conclusions were initially not seen as too radical, as the persons who initiated the new perspective are viewed not as outsiders but respected colleagues since they themselves taught for a lengthy period the older version of dispensationalism. Their methodologies are far more sophisticated, though their abilities as theologians are not necessarily more sophisticated, since many within the older position had advanced degrees, years of teaching and research experience, and were widely known and respected. However, it could be argued that they had simply accepted the received dispensational tradition and had not critically reflected upon many of the key issues, such as the interpretation of the Davidic covenant and its many implications. Certainly, this conclusion cannot be stated concerning those who initiated the new version of dispensationalism; they thought more deeply especially about the hermeneutical foundations of classical dispensationalism. Some argue that their conclusions have so radically altered the received tradition that their perspective is no longer within the ranks of dispensationalism while others believe the adjustments are not too extreme. Some argue that their views really are not new at all but are very similar to other scholars' conclusions, such as George E. Ladd.

Conclusion

THE INTERPRETATION OF THE New Testament doctrine of the kingdom has historically led to a variety of conclusions. The amillennial position is the most prominent within Christianity, holding prominence within the church from the time of Augustine to the period of the Reformation. Daniel Whitby, in the eighteenth century, is usually credited as being the father of postmillennialism. This position held a highly optimistic view of the flow of history. This position eventually faded due to tragic world events such as World War I, the Great Depression, and World War II. This view held that the kingdom would come gradually, especially through the preaching and reception of the claims of the gospel throughout the world. The views of the second coming and the general judgment were very similar to the amillennial position. Weber offers insight into postmillennialism, stating,

> This view places the Second Coming *after* a long period of gradual and incremental "Gospel Success" in which the vast majority of humanity is converted to Christ and human society is radically reformed. This transformation will occur through the Holy Spirit using the "ordinary means of grace." Thus, this perspective is inherently optimistic about the course of history and the power of preaching, teaching, evangelism, and social reform to bring about permanent change. Adherents expect evil to be drastically reduced during the millennium, but not completely eliminated. Postmillennialists refer to various biblical texts, including some premillennial favorites (e.g., Isaiah 2 and Micah 4). The parables of the mustard seed and yeast (Matt 13) show the kingdom's gradual development and penetrating power. Likewise, Jesus' power over the demonic Powers has proved that "the kingdom of God has come upon you" (Matt 12:28). After his resurrection, Jesus announced

that he had been given all authority in heaven and on earth (Matt 28:18); and at his ascension he sat down at God's right hand as king (Acts 2:22–36). Post millennialists use both a preterist and historicist approach to apocalyptic passages. Concerning Revelation 20, they argue that a "thousand" is a figurative number that stands for the golden age that will be established by the power of the gospel over time. . . . This view has been especially popular among Reformed Christians.[1]

The early church held to a premillennial understanding—that is, Christ would return and then set up his kingdom; however, there was no understanding that there would be a rapture or translation of the church before the second advent of Christ. Weber states,

> Apocalyptic millennialism was widespread in the first three centuries, thanks in large part to Papias, a second-century bishop whose views influenced many others. Justin Martyr taught the rise of the Antichrist, the great tribulation, the return of Christ, the first resurrection, a "thousand years in Jerusalem," then a second resurrection followed by the judgment (*Dialogue with Trypho*, 80–81, 110). Irenaeus taught a similar prophetic scenario, drawing heavily on prophetic and apocalyptic texts from both testaments (*Against Heresies*, V.25–36). Though a fierce opponent of anything considered nonorthodox, Tertullian combined common views about the Parousia, the first resurrection, and the thousand-year kingdom.[2]

Though many believe that dispensationalism is a new movement in theology, dating back to only the mid-nineteenth century with the writings of John Nelson Darby, there is credible evidence of a semblance of an earlier foundation for this method of interpretation. Arnold Ehlert compiled an extensive bibliography that he believes gives credence to the belief that there was a semblance of dispensationalism, though not called by this term, in the church fathers as well as in the writings of both John Edwards and Jonathan Edwards.

Classical dispensationalism is believed to have been initiated by John Nelson Darby as contained in his thirty-two-volume work entitled *The Collected Writings of J. N. Darby*. The positions of both Scofield and Chafer were like those of Darby. Scofield is recognized more for his extensive Bible study notes while Chafer is more academically oriented and was especially

---

1. Weber, "Millennialism," 367–68.
2. Weber, "Millennialism," 369.

known for his *Systematic Theology*. Chafer died in 1952; his long legacy of classical dispensational interpretation was heavily influential for the following four decades until the introduction of progressive dispensationalism.

The newer position of progressive dispensationalism seemingly has many similarities with the position of historic premillennialism; there is in both a literal interpretation of both Old and New Testament passages emphasizing that world conditions will not gradually improve but will worsen until the second advent occurs and the establishing of the earthly millennial kingdom. This perspective is seen in the writings of many of the church fathers who predate Augustine. Progressive dispensationalism, however, places more emphasis upon the Davidic covenant and the position that Christ is seated on the Davidic throne presently, ruling and ordering matters pertaining to humanity, the church, and the world.

Many of the early dispensationalists were indoctrinated in Reformed theology and were ordained within denominations and communions of this theological persuasion. Many of the basic tenets of progressive dispensationalism have seemingly moved back either into or very close to this theological position. Progressive dispensationalists use what is termed a "complementary hermeneutic" along with a literal hermeneutic.[3] Most significantly, they believe that the kingdom promises are occurring in the present since Christ is reigning now on the throne of David; they claim, though, the final fulfillment of those promises will only be realized in the future millennial kingdom.

Wesleyan theology was never a theological position accepted by dispensationalists since there were major differences concerning a variety of issues. This is on account of the fact of the Reformed influence, which is predominant especially within early dispensationalism. Dispensationalists, for example, unlike adherents of Wesleyan theology, believe in the perseverance of the saints—that is, when one has experienced true grace, one will not lose that relationship. The belief in prevenient grace was never a part of dispensational teaching since dispensational theology holds that the human will is bound and subject to sin and is not able to humanly decide for grace; divine intervention is necessary, they believe. The issues of election and the extent of the atonement are a matter of debate, but the consensus is that the atonement is not limited to only the elect. However, the Princeton theologians are widely read and many of their basic assumptions and tenets are accepted by especially the early dispensationalists.

3. Ryrie, *Dispensationalism*, 189–210.

DAVIDIC MILLENNIALISM

Progressive dispensationalists greatly modified classic dispensationalism. They have moved in the distinct direction of a return to historic premillennialism; however, the new theological position is still within the ranks of dispensationalism. The criticism leveled against the theological position historically, especially by Reformed theologians, is not as strong as in the past since the new position borders on a Reformed position. The name dispensationalism, however, still evokes a negative connotation with many, and in a sense may even be confusing; therefore, the new name Davidic millennialism seems to be more appropriate for the theological position of those who are progressive dispensationalists.

The progressive dispensationalists, however, seemingly have some postmillennialism nuances to their theological position. The position is more optimistic than classic dispensationalism. It is obvious that progressive dispensationalism has moved toward a more Reformed understanding of the kingdom.

The different conceptions of the kingdom within classical dispensationalism and progressive dispensationalism has not previously been clearly outlined. This work has outlined the differences, viewing both the continuity and discontinuity of the interpretations of what constitutes the New Testament word kingdom. Given these differences, the proposal is that another nomenclature rather than progressive dispensationalism is necessary. Both the classical and progressive perspectives place the culmination of the kingdom with the seating of Christ on the throne of David. However, given progressive dispensationalism's position that the kingdom is active in this age, and taking into account 1 Cor. 5:28, which states that in eternity, the Father has all sovereignty since Christ will, out of obedience, grant the kingdom to him, finally fulfilling the Davidic covenant, the name Davidic millennialism rather than progressive dispensationalism is appropriate.

Jesus and His reign is anticipated by all serious Christians. His genealogy is given in detail in Matthew 1:6-16; he is given the title "Son of David" at least seventeen times in the New Testament alone. Matthew 15:22 records that the Cananite woman cries out: "Have mercy on me, O Lord, Son of David." The apostle Paul claims in Romans 1:3 that Jesus descends from David in the flesh. John quotes Jesus' words in Revelation 22:16 stating: "I am the root and descendant of David, the bright and morning star." All of human history is fulfilled totally in His completed and sovereign reign.

Davidic millennialism is revisionary for three essential reasons: 1. the emphasis is placed upon redemption, which can be argued to be the major

CONCLUSION

theme of the Bible; 2. the term unifies both the Old and New Testaments; 3. Davidic millennialism places the emphasis upon Christ, the ultimate annointed One.

Bibliography

Ahlstrom, Sydney. *A Religious History of the American People.* 2 vols. Garden City, NY: Doubleday, 1975.

Aland, Kurt, et al., eds. *The Greek New Testament.* Stuttgart: Württemberg Bible Society, 1968.

Allis, Oswald T. "Modern Dispensationalism and the Doctrine of the Unity of the Scriptures." *Evangelical Quarterly* 8 (Jan. 1936) 22–35.

———. "Modern Dispensationalism and the Law of God." *Evangelical Quarterly* 8 (July 1936) 272–89.

———. *Prophecy and the Church.* Philadelphia: P&R, 1945.

Augustine. *The City of God.* New York: Penguin, 1981.

Barth, Karl. *The Epistle to the Romans.* Translated by Edwyn C. Hoskyns. Oxford: Oxford University Press, 1933.

Bass, Clarence. *Backgrounds to Dispensationalism.* Grand Rapids: Eerdmans, 1960.

Bear, James E. "Dispensationalism and the Covenant of Grace." *Union Seminary Review* 49 (July 1939) 285–307.

Blaising, Craig A., and Darrell L. Bock. *Progressive Dispensationalism.* Grand Rapids: Baker, 2000.

Bock, Darrell L. "Hermeneutics of Progressive Dispensationalism." In *Three Central Issues in Contemporary Dispensationalism*, edited by Herbert W. Bateman IV. Grand Rapids: Kregel Publications, 1999.

Bowman, John Wick. "Dispensationalism." *Interpretation* 10 (Apr. 1956) 170–86.

Brown, Harold O. J. *Heresies: Heresy and Orthodoxy in the History of the Church.* Peabody, MA: Hendrickson, 1988.

Chafer, Lewis Sperry. "Are There Two Ways to Be Saved?" *Bibliotheca Sacra* 105 (Jan. 1948) 1.

———. "Dispensational Distinctives Challenged." *Bibliotheca Sacra* 100 (July 1943) 337.

———. "Dispensationalism." *Bibliotheca Sacra* 93 (Oct. 1936) 410.

———. *Dispensationalism.* Rev. ed. Dallas: Dallas Seminary Press, 1951.

———. Foreword to *Millennialism: The Two Major Views*, by Charles L. Feinberg. Reprint, Chicago: Moody, 1980.

———. "The Future of the Gentiles." *Moody Monthly* 4 (Nov. 1940) 155–56.

———. *Grace: The Glorious Theme.* Grand Rapids: Zondervan, 1950.

———. "An Introduction to the Study of Prophecy." *Bibliotheca Sacra* 100 (Jan. 1943) 108–9.
———. "Inventing Heretics Through Misunderstanding." *Bibliotheca Sacra* 102 (Jan. 1945) 1.
———. *The Kingdom in History and Prophecy*. Reprint, Philadelphia: Sunday School Times, 1926.
———. *Major Bible Themes*. Rev. ed. Grand Rapids: Dunham, 1964.
———. *Satan*. Rev. ed. Grand Rapids: Zondervan, 1977.
———. *Systematic Theology*. 8 vols. Dallas: Dallas Seminary Press, 1937–48.
———. "Twenty Years of Experience." *Bulletin of Dallas Theological Seminary* 29 (July–Sept. 1943) 3.
———. "What I Learned from Dr. Scofield." *Sunday School Times* 64 (Mar. 1922) 120.
———. "What Will God Do with the Cosmos?" In *Light for the World's Darkness*, edited by John W. Bradbury. New York: Loizeaux Brothers, 1944.
Clouse, Robert G. "Fundamentalist Theology." In *The Oxford Handbook of Eschatology*, edited by Jerry L. Walls. New York: Oxford University Press, 2008.
Darby, J. N. *The Collected Writings of J. N. Darby*. 47 vols. Dublin: G. Morrish, 1879–83.
Ehlert, Arnold. "A Bibliography of Dispensationalism." *Bibliotheca Sacra* 101 (Jan. 1944) 95–101.
Elwell, Walter A. "Dispensationalism of the Third Kind." *Christianity Today*, Sept. 12, 1994.
English, E. Schuyler. *Re-Thinking the Rapture*. Rev. ed. Neptune, NJ: Loizeaux Brothers, 1970.
Erickson, Millard. *Christian Theology*. Grand Rapids: Baker Academic, 1999.
Gaebelein, A. C. *The Conflict of the Ages*. Reprint, Neptune, NJ: Loizeaux Brothers, 1983.
———. *The Prophet Daniel*. Rev. ed. Grand Rapids: Kregel, 1955.
———. *The Revelation*. Reprint, Neptune, NJ: Loizeaux Brothers, 1961.
———. *World Prospects: How Is It All Going to End?* New York: Our Hope, 1934.
Grant, James. *The Plymouth Brethren: Their History and Heresies*. London: William Macintosh, 1875.
Grudem, Wayne. *Systematic Theology: An Introduction to Biblical Doctrine*. 2nd ed. Grand Rapids: Zondervan Academic, 2000.
Harnack, Adolph von. *What Is Christianity?* Translated by Thomas Saunders. London: Williams & Norgate, 1904.
Hodge, Archibald Alexander. *Outlines of Theology*. Rev ed. New York: A. C. Armstrong & Son, 1895.
Hodge, Charles. *Systematic Theology: Soteriology*. Vol. 3. Reprint, Grand Rapids: Eerdmans, 1940.
Hodges, Zane. "A Dispensational Understanding of Acts 2." In *Issues in Dispensationalism*, edited by Wesley R. Willis and John R. Master. Chicago: Moody, 1847.
Hoekema, Anthony A. *The Bible and the Future*. Grand Rapids: Eerdmans, 1979.
Ice, Thomas D. "A Short History of Dispensationalism." Liberty University Article Archives 37 (May 2009) 1–10. https://digitalcommons.liberty.edu/pretrib_arch/37.
Ironside, H. A. *Isaiah*. Neptune, NJ: Loizeaux Brothers, 1952.
———. *Not Wrath but Rapture*. 2nd ed. Neptune, NJ: Loizeaux Brothers, 1988.
Kelly, William. *Lectures on the Gospel of Matthew*. Rev. ed. London: Pickering & Inglis, n.d.
Ladd, George Elden. *Crucial Questions About the Kingdom of God*. Grand Rapids: Eerdmans, 1952.

BIBLIOGRAPHY

———. *A Theology of the New Testament*. Grand Rapids: Eerdmans, 1974.
Landrum, Lynn. "Thinking Out Loud." *Dallas Morning News*, July 13, 1948.
Lincoln, C. F. "Biographical Sketch of the Author." In vol. 8 of *Systematic Theology: Biographical Sketches and Indexes*, by Lewis Sperry Chafer. Dallas: Dallas Seminary Press, 1948.
MacCulloch, David. *The Reformation*. London: Penguin, 2004.
Mackintosh, C. H. *The Mackintosh Treasury: Miscellaneous Writings*. Neptune, NJ: Loizeaux Brothers, 1898.
Marsden, George M. *Fundamentalism and American Culture*. New York: Oxford University Press, 1980.
Mason, Clarence, Jr. "A Readable and Thrilling Theology." *Our Hope* 55 (Mar. 1949) 535.
Moody, Dale. "Present Theological Trends: A Review Article." *Review and Expositor* 47.1 (1950) 9–11.
Payne, J. Barton. *The Imminent Appearing of Christ*. Grand Rapids: Eerdmans, 1962.
Peters, George N. H. *The Theocratic Kingdom*. 3 vols. Reprint, Grand Rapids: Kregel Ministry, 1952.
Pettingill, William L. *Simple Studies in Matthew*. Harrisburg: Fred Kelker, 1910.
Poythress, Vern S. *Understanding Dispensationalists*. 2nd ed. Phillipsburg, NJ: P&R, 1994.
Renfer, Rudolf A. "A History of Dallas Theological Seminary." PhD diss., University of Texas, Austin, 1959.
Robertson, O. Palmer. *The Christ of the Covenants*. Grand Rapids: Baker, 1980.
Rowland, Christopher. "The Eschatology of the New Testament." In *The Oxford Handbook of Eschatology*, edited by Jerry L. Walls. New York: Oxford University Press, 2008.
Ryrie, Charles. *The Basis of the Premillennial Faith*. New York: Loizeaux Brothers, 1953.
———. *Dispensationalism*. Chicago: Moody, 2007.
Sandeen, Ernest. *The Roots of Fundamentalism*. Grand Rapids: Baker, 1978.
Saucy, Robert L. *The Case for Progressive Dispensationalism*. Grand Rapids: Zondervan, 1993.
———. "The Church as the Mystery of God." In *Dispensationalism, Israel and the Church*, edited by Craig A. Blaising and Darrell L. Bock. Grand Rapids: Zondervan, 1992.
Scofield, C. I. *Addresses on Prophecy*. New York: A. C. Gaebelein, 1919.
———. Introduction to *The Kingdom in History and Prophecy*, by Lewis Sperry Chafer. Reprint, Philadelphia: Sunday School Times, 1926.
———. *Rightly Dividing the Word of Truth*. Neptune, NJ: Loizeaux Brothers, 1896.
———, ed. *The Scofield Reference Bible*. New York: Oxford University Press, 1909.
———. *What Do the Prophets Say?* Philadelphia: Sunday School Times, 1918.
Toussaint, Stanley D. "The Contingency of the Coming Kingdom." In *Integrity of Heart, Skillfulness of Hands*, edited by Charles H. Dyer and Roy B. Zuck. Grand Rapids: Baker, 1994.
Virkler, Henry A., and Karelynne Gerber Ayayo. *Hermeneutics: Principles and Processes of Biblical Interpretation*. Grand Rapids: Baker Academic, 2007.
Vivano, Benedict T. "Eschatology and the Quest for the Historical Jesus." In *The Oxford Handbook of Eschatology*, edited by Jerry L. Walls. New York: Oxford University Press, 2008.
Walls, Jerry L., ed. *The Oxford Handbook of Eschatology*. New York: Oxford University Press, 2008.
Walvoord, John F. "Lewis Sperry Chafer." *Sunday School Times* 94 (Oct. 11, 1952) 869.

BIBLIOGRAPHY

———. Review of *Systematic Theology*, by Lewis Sperry Chafer. *Bibliotheca Sacra* 105 (Jan. 1948) 115.

Warfield, Benjamin B. "The Gospel and the Second Coming." In *Selected Shorter Writings of Benjamin B. Warfield*, edited by John E. Meeter. Nutley, NJ: P&R, 1973.

———. "The Millennium and the Apocalypse." *Princeton Theological Review* 2 (Oct. 1904) 601.

Weber, Timothy. *Living in the Shadow of the Second Coming*. Grand Rapids: Zondervan, 1983.

———. "Millennialism." In *The Oxford Handbook of Eschatology*, edited by Jerry L. Walls. New York: Oxford University Press, 2008.

www.ingramcontent.com/pod-product-compliance
Lightning Source LLC
Chambersburg PA
CBHW071442160426
43195CB00013B/2008